Damn the Torpedoes!

Damn the Torpedoes!

AND MORE TALES OF LIVEABOARD LIFE

Catherine Dook

TouchWood Editions Ltd.
Victoria, BC, Canada.
This book is distributed by The Heritage Group, #108-17665 66A Avenue, Surrey, BC, Canada, V3S 2A7.

Cover design by Pat McCallum; book design by Retta Moorman; layout by Darlene Nickull. Cover images: Front, Jean-Paul Briand; back, Tania Strauss. This book is set in AGaramond.

TouchWood Editions acknowledges the financial support for its publishing program from the Canada Council for the Arts, the Government of Canada through the Book Publishing Industry Development Program (BPIDP) and the Province of British Columbia through the British Columbia Arts Council.

Printed and bound in Canada by Friesens, Altona, Manitoba.

National Library of Canada Cataloguing in Publication

Dook, Catherine, 1954-
   Damn the torpedoes!: and more tales of liveaboard life / Catherine Dook.
— 1st ed.

   ISBN 1-894898-06-0

   1. Dook, Catherine, 1954-   . 2. Sailing — Humour. I. Title.
GV777.3.D658 2003   797.1'24'0207   C2003-910335-8

The Canada Council | Le Conseil des Arts
for the Arts | du Canada

BRITISH
COLUMBIA
ARTS COUNCIL

Dedicated to my grandmother,
Mary Beaton Parsons,
born 1905,
and my friend,
Endis Felix,
1975-2001.
"Some sailed over the ocean in ships."

Acknowledgments

Many of these stories first appeared in *South Cowichan Life, Boat Journal* and *Nor'Westing* magazines.

I wish to thank Pat Touchie, whose vision extends beyond my spelling, grammar and typing, and Marlyn Horsdal, my editor. I am deeply grateful for her excellent input, without which I would not write right.

I would like to thank the two fine young men who were the inspiration for the story "Stupendous Man." The first is Jeremy Wilson, the budding author who invented the character Stupendous Man; he still has the freckles but his mother (the evil Mom Lady) got him a haircut as soon as the story was published in *Boat Journal*. Myron Dion, then president of the student union, was guilty, guilty, guilty of every classroom transgression mentioned in the story. The day his alarm clock went off just before the recess bell, I darn near had a heart attack. I've never laughed as heartily since Jeremy and Myron.

Thank you to all our neighbours. You are wonderful people and we esteem you greatly — for your humour, your kindness, your willingness to give us advice and tow us home and, above all, for your tolerance of us.

Those readers who enjoyed the first book and said so are greatly appreciated.

My children and grandchildren have encouraged and supported me, as have my parents, Brock and Mary Parsons. Lisa, Maggie, Jackie, Rupert, John Jr. and Paul, nobody could ask for better progeny.

And, of course, thank you, my darling John. You are the best, and I love you.

Catherine Dook
2003

Contents

Introduction

"The reason you didn't win the Giller Prize," John said, "is because the Giller Prize is for fiction."

"Well, you know newspaper photographers," my neighbour said. "He just caught you at a bad angle."

"Hardly anybody ever comes to the first signing," said the bookstore owner. "It takes time to gain momentum."

"Catherine who?" said the lady at the book warehouse.

"Have you got spellcheck on your computer yet?" asked my publisher.

"You've been honoured by everybody," said my grandma. "Are you writing a sequel?"

That's all the encouragement I needed. After all, tons of exciting stuff had happened to John and me onboard the *Inuksuk* since the first book, *"Darling, Call the Coast Guard, We're on Fire Again!"* We'd moved the boat to Sooke, lured by the promise of a regular paycheque. We left behind our friends at Cowichan Bay, none of whom were speaking to us because we'd had a little problem with cockroaches. (See first book.) Once in Sooke, well, read on and enjoy.

Grandma, this one's for you.

Letter to Cowichan Bay

Dᴇᴀʀ Cᴏᴡɪᴄʜᴀɴ Bᴀʏ Dock-Dwellers,
Greetings! You can stand down from your radios now — we pulled into Sooke Harbour a week ago! Thanks for lending us Jean-Paul and Endis and little Angelique — we figured since they'd made it safely from Vanuatu in the South Pacific, a little jaunt from Cowichan Bay to Sooke would be a piece of cake. But after we'd sailed a bit, we wondered how Jean-Paul had made it to the South Pacific without Endis. The trip back we understood, because she'd been there to give him advice. But how did he make it down there? It isn't just that he has one artificial hand, an untidy ponytail and a gleam in his eye, because he can tie a bow line with his good hand, keep things shipshape and man the wheel with dexterity. But he seems to have a little trouble steering.

Endis is at home on the deck of a boat. She is lithe and graceful and unafraid. She can read a chart at a glance, plot a course, program a GPS, haul a line and give a considered, intelligent, first mate's opinion. All at the same time. Then she offers to help me in the galley, amuses Angelique for an hour and stands sturdily behind the wheel with the sun on her enraptured face, steering the course straight as true love. Jean-Paul is a reliable, competent South Sea veteran, but Endis has talent.

Doggedly I followed her out on the deck — on my hands and knees. Doggedly I pulled on lines and doggedly I peered into the bowels of the ocean from a crouching position, though darned if I knew what I was looking for.

"Jean-Paul! Kelp bed!" Endis said sharply, and "Jean-Paul! Rocks, one o'clock!"

My job was to cook massive pressure-cooker meals at four-hour intervals. Angelique, only three, danced impatiently in the cockpit. We motor-sailed past Sidney, waved at D'Arcy Island and bucked currents around Trial Island. As the bow swung, "Jean-Paul!" Endis said, "stay the course."

We tied up in Victoria for the night, then tackled Race Passage at slack tide the next day and holed up in Becher Bay for a nap while the tide turned in our favour. Out of Becher Bay the fog was thick as soup. John gave me the job of ringing the bell, and I did so well he begged me to stop after only half an hour of dingings every 15 seconds. He had kind of an anguished look about him, but it may have been because the GPS was dancing us around the chart, or because we had to rely heavily on the radar, or perhaps it was because the current kept swinging us out to sea. Or it may have been because he'd eaten two days' worth of my special offshore cooking. Whatever it was, he looked worse when Secretary Island loomed at us out of the fog, 40 feet off our bow and moving closer at five knots.

"Jean-Paul!" said Endis.

"Hard to port!" John yelled. For sheer lack of knowing what to do, I rang the bell. Luck was on our side. We dodged around Secretary Island, nearly rammed the lighthouse ("Jean-Paul!" Endis said. "What are you doing?") and neatly avoided Whiffin Spit by a hair. ("Jean-Paul!" Endis said.) It was with considerable relief that we saw there was less fog in Sooke Harbour. Then our depth sounder let loose with an anguished mechanical cry, and crab pots sprang about our bow like bobbing bathtub toys.

"Jean-Paul!" Endis said. We consulted the GPS, which revealed we were *not* in the channel on the way to Sooke Basin — something Endis and I had suspected after we nearly nailed the first six crab pots. We lost one of the dinghy's oars and as we swung the boat wildly in an effort to retrieve it, we missed another ten crab pots and ended up in water so shallow I wanted to wade to shore. Endis scooped up the oar with one graceful swipe from the dinghy. We found the channel, or something close to it, and then spotted the entrance to Sooke Basin; we chugged across it with light hearts and a silent depth sounder.

When we docked, the wind sweeping down the mountain and across Sooke Basin caught us broadside, the boat swung out bow first and Jean-Paul jumped from the stern. "Jean-Paul!" Endis said. He secured the stern line first and then the spring, but he had to fight the wind, which had caught the boat. I threw the bow line. John was terribly proud of me.

You see, my skills are more linguistic than nautical. My specialties lie in ringing bells, firing up the pressure cooker and giving advice. But I aspire to achieve the competence of Endis, who can handle a boat with the skill of a master, and whose warning rings through the fog like a bell — "Jean-Paul!"

May your masts always point skyward.

Love,
Catherine

P.S. It wasn't until later we found out that without his glasses Jean-Paul is as blind as a bat.

Ampless in Sooke

"FIFTEEN AMPS?" I said. "Whaddya mean 15 amps?"

"Well, that's all there is at this marina," said John.

"So what's the problem?" I asked. "Sooke not up to the finer points of electricity, or what?"

"Don't be snotty," said John. "Lots of marinas have only 15 amps."

"And just when I was getting used to refrigeration," I sighed. "Will we still be able to run the electric head, or will we be forced to use a bucket? Tell me the worst immediately, darling — I can take it. I might mention it now and then — you know — in passing, and I might telephone my 48 intimate friends, and then e-mail another 20 or so in case I missed anyone and just drop it into the conversation, but ..."

"Oh — that reminds me," said John. "We'll have to use a cell phone. That means no long-distance calls out and no e-mail either."

"What?" I gasped, falling back onto the settee, too stunned to speak for a moment. "It's every woman's inalienable right to get e-mail and talk to her 48 best friends on the phone."

"It's easily 600 feet down the dock to the power," said John. "It's too far to run a phone line. And nobody else is hooked up. We only have one neighbour."

"Where's the fun in having one neighbour?" I said. "You need at least two neighbours so two of you can talk about the one who's not there."

"Well, there's lots of seals and weekend boaters," said John.

"Weekend boaters don't stop to chat," I said. "And the seals smell like rotting fish. And they stare."

"The seals or the boaters?" asked John.

"Both," I said. "Especially when I stand on the dock and practise my seal-calling techniques. I've noticed the tourists look even more interested than the seals."

"Frightened too," said John. "And can you blame them? It's not every day a fat lady blocks the dock and hoots at the seals sunning on the breakwater."

"Yes it is," I said. "I'm out there every morning after breakfast."

"Surely you can find something different to do with your time," said John.

"Well," I said, "seeing as how we have no ladies in the neighbourhood to swap husband stories with, maybe I can take up watching TV."

"Actually, no," said John. "We only get two channels, and we don't even get radio reception when our neighbour uses his power tools."

"Fifteen amps," I moaned. "Fate has nailed me for all the times I whined about our 30 amps in Cowichan Bay. I was bathed in a luxurious sea of whirring appliances then, disturbed only by the odd retort as I blew the breakers. But here ..." I paused to gaze sweepingly around the galley, "I dare not even attempt toast and hot water at the same time. Mornings we'll sit around in our underwear and discuss what comes first — sustenance or cleanliness. If we blow the dock breakers here, one of us will have to get dressed and walk 600 feet down the dock in the rain to reset the breakers, and even though I love you, it's not going to be me."

"You sound a little cranky," said John.

"Cranky!" I said. "Cranky! We've been here two days, right? Well, we got our mail forwarded today, and some evil person put my name on a promotion for a free seniors' magazine. I spent the morning reading about makeup tips for wrinkled skin. The cover girl was wearing bifocals. Then, to add insult to injury, the young man at the local pharmacy told me today was Senior Citizen Monday. He's lucky I let him live."

"Well, I have some good news," said John.

"What?" I sniffed.

John drew me into his arms and hugged me. "The 15 amps here can handle our battery charger just fine, and you may have unlimited use of the head."

I gasped out loud. "Darling!" I exclaimed, and melted into his arms. "I'll get on the computer immediately and do a mass mailing to my 68 friends to let them know. And the water pump? Can I run the water-pressure pump too? And can I make coffee in the electric drip coffee pot?"

"Of course, my little Snoggy Lips," said John. "But don't be greedy — if you expect head time AND fresh coffee, you'll have to type by candlelight."

I sighed contentedly. "Well, perhaps 15 amps isn't so bad after all. I look much younger and thinner in dim light."

The Excursion

"TODAY'S THE DAY we change marinas from Sooke Basin to Sooke Harbour," said John.

"We'd better go grocery shopping," I said.

"Whatever for?" asked my husband.

"Provisions, darling," I said.

"Don't be ridiculous," said John. "The trip will take only about an hour and a half down the harbour."

"That's what you say now, my love," I said. "You'll change your tune when the current swings us off course and we tangle the prop in a crab-pot line and we're grounded and we have to order takeout from Sooke Harbour House until I max out my VISA a week later. I wonder if they deliver by dinghy? We'll need provisions when we run out of money."

"Hmnph," said John.

"Let's see now," I said. "Five kilos of flour, two kilos of sugar, a couple of cans of coffee, half a dozen cans of milk, two roasts and some pork chops, a sack of potatoes and enough propane to last us a week. Our canned provisions should hold out for a while, and we have a bunch of bananas and a sack of apples." I finished my list with a flourish. "With luck," I said, "we should be hung up only five or six days eating takeout before the local coast guard auxiliary can find a vessel big enough to drag us out of trouble." I sighed with happiness. "It's been so long since we've eaten out. I understand Mom's Café serves first-rate food too. That nice couple at Juan's has bait and crab traps. If we're hung up I bet there'll be crabs all around us. We'll eat like kings." I wrapped my arms around John and gave him a hug. "You plan the best trips, darling," I said. Then I hurried off.

When I returned with sacks of groceries, John was standing on the deck impatiently undoing and refastening lines.

"Hurry up," he said. "We cast off in half an hour."

The wind was pushing the *Inuksuk* away from the dock. The sky was painted with a tracing of cirrus clouds and the sun was bright and nearly warm. I put on my cruiser suit and climbed onto the deck.

"Fluorescent orange isn't my colour, darling," I said. "Why don't they make cruiser suits in gold or russet or olive green?"

"Hold onto the bow line," said John, "and release it when I yell. I'm going to reverse us out of here."

"Aye, captain," I replied. "Maybe a co-ordinating set of earmuffs would mute the ensemble, or gloves in an earth tone. You should have given me another half-hour to shop."

"Time and tide wait for no man," said John. "Any more delays, and you'll be demoted from first mate to dhobi wallah without pay."

He pressed the starter.

The throbbing roar of the engine sent all the seals hurtling from the breakwater where they'd been peacefully sunning, and squawking seagulls rose in a patterned mass. Our neighbour came out of his boat to say goodbye.

"Come with us," I cried. Visions of not having to leap to the dock flashed through my brain. Waddling slightly, I walked to the side of the boat, my cruiser suit swishing loudly. "We could use the help docking," I said.

Our neighbour swung himself onboard. "Sure," he said.

We cast off the lines. The wind caught the stern while I stood poised on the deck holding the bow line. I released the line and quickly pulled it in, dripping and cold. The men conferred in the cockpit while I tidied lines, and then I made my way back to the bow, alert for crab pots, icebergs and the edge of the world. The wind whipped my hair. I spread my arms. "I'm flying," I yelled. I felt like Kate Winslet without the wardrobe consultant. I felt wonderful.

We threaded our way cautiously down the harbour. There was the occasional crab-pot sighting, but mostly, it struck me, the crab pots were in quantity to starboard. I made my way back to the cockpit. "Darling," I said, "how come we encountered a zillion crab pots on the way into the harbour a month ago and there are hardly any on the way out? How come our depth sounder yelled at us all the way in and it's not making a peep on the way out? Could it be …" I paused. "John," I said, "did we follow the channel markers on our way into Sooke Basin a month ago?"

"Of course, my little dumpling," said John. "We were just on the wrong side of them, is all." He grinned at me and returned to his wheel.

I picked my way to the bow, joyous of heart. Sooke Harbour was possible! Knowing the magic formula unlocked the door to endless wonders — like weekend excursions, sailing, fishing and a prop forever free of crab-pot lines. We'd had only one neighbour, but he knew where the channel was. He was as magical as Harry Potter. I glanced back. Why, our old marina was just a short drive from the new one. Perhaps he'd be willing to come sailing with us on sunny days.

The *Inuksuk* docked as neatly as a ballerina. John really was getting expert. A friendly-looking man caught our lines, we tied up and everyone celebrated with a round of coffee.

"You know, darling," I said to John later, "you are terribly clever. It's okay that we didn't get to eat takeout. And we should have a really nice supper tonight. Luckily, we have lots of provisions."

Stupendous Man

I'T'S BEEN A terrible week. Already I can see the cumulus clouds of discontent looming over our yacht. The winds of change are sweeping through the rigging. The rain of sorrow is streaming down the mast and gathering in little puddles in the cockpit, where I've stored two suitcases full of books, trying to shield them from the wharf rats. Futile! Futile! Futile! The wharf rats are winning, the boat is dripping and our little heater is struggling valiantly to suck juice through a narrow 15-amp cord. The thermometer registers 16 degrees Fahrenheit. I shiver and take a cup of coffee on the deck. Tears of rain slop into my little mug. I stand in the wet and look up at the weeping sky. "Why, oh Lord," I ask, "did I ever agree to teach Grade Seven?"

There is no answer — just the steady drip of rain and a sigh of wind. Of course! There is no answer! Down through the ages, teachers have never coped with Grade Seven — at least, not successfully. When Socrates complained about the youth of his day, he was describing Grade Seven. The 12-year-old cabin boys who ran away to sea — why, they were Grade Seven students. Any Grade Seven boy would prefer rats and weevils to the rigours of language arts. Young girls who got married in the Middle Ages were escaping Grade Seven math, and the spelling test on Friday. The village idiot used to be a schoolteacher, poor mad soul, and the ship's captain who spent years at sea torn from his loved ones had junior high children.

I returned to the main saloon. "Let's go sailing," I said to my husband. "Let's go sailing."

"It's pouring rain," said John.

"Oh," I said. "So it is." I sighed.

I heard a voice from outside. "Hi — Mrs. Dook!"

I grabbed my husband's arm. "It's one of my students! It's Trevor! Hide me!"

"Whatever for?" asked my husband. "He's only a kid."

"You haven't met Trevor," I gasped. "Even his parents are frightened of him."

"Don't be silly," said John. "Invite him in."

Reluctantly, I poked my head up through the main passageway. Standing jauntily on the dock in the rain was a 12-year-old boy with wild hair and freckles. "Hi, Mrs. Dook," he said. "I came to visit."

"Yeah?" I said suspiciously. "How'd you get past the locked gate?"

"I remembered everything you taught us about random numbers," he said proudly. "Only took me 20 minutes."

"Oh," I said. "Do you have that foot-long pencil with you — the one you told me yesterday was your only writing instrument?"

"No," he said.

"Got any gum or candy or that licorice you said your doctor prescribed?"

"No."

"Did you bring your remote-control car with the switch that won't shut off?"

"No."

"The alarm clock set for recess?"

"No."

"Any misspelled notes saying you're not allowed to have detention?"

"No."

"Then come aboard," I said.

Trevor hopped gracefully into the cockpit and clambered down the ladder. "Neat boat," he said, glancing around the main saloon. "Do you and Mr. Dook ever get lonely here?"

"No, never," I said quickly.

"Lots of seals around here," Trevor said. "Do they belong to anybody?"

"Well, not me," I said, glancing at my watch. I handed him a Coke. "Does your mother expect you?"

"You mean the evil Mom-Lady?" asked Trevor. "She attempted to cramp the style of Stupendous Man, so he fled out the door to escape her clutches. Stupendous Man wants to go to sea." He paused. "You know," he said confidingly, "sometimes I get into trouble at home." He looked pensively down at his Coke.

John spoke up. "It's pouring rain," he said helplessly. "Nobody can run away to sea today."

"Surely Stupendous Man can talk to the evil Mom-Lady," I said. "Stupendous Man has super negotiating powers. Stupendous Man can con the evil Teacher-Lady into extra recess and make her laugh in mid-yell."

"The evil Teacher-Lady is not as smart as the evil Mom-Lady," he said sadly. "No offence."

"None taken," I said kindly. "You know, Trevor, sometimes I've felt like running away to sea too. This week, in fact."

"You have?" he asked.

"Sure," I said. "How would you like to come sailing with us some sunny day?"

"Sounds great," he said, jumping to his feet. "Can I bring my mom?"

"Of course," I said.

"Have to go now," he said, and scampered up the ladder. Through the splashing rain, I could hear his voice trail back. "Hey Mrs. Dook! I bet Mom would like a baby seal as a present. Help me catch one?"

I turned to John. "Grade Seven!" I said.

The Fresh Breeze

Iᴛ ᴡᴀs ɴɪɢʜᴛ in Sooke Harbour. John and I were alone onboard the *Inuksuk* surrounded by a hundred empty fishing boats. "Listen to that wind howl," I remarked to my husband. "The rigging is a-roaring. I wonder how strong the wind is."

John disappeared up the companionway with his hand-held windmeter. He clambered back down the ladder, slammed the hatch cover and raced a pencil over a scrap of paper, pursing his lips and frowning. He looked up triumphantly.

"It's not serious," he said. "According to my calculations, this is a fresh breeze."

There was a great roar, the boat threw herself into the dock and six books shot onto the floor with a thud, tangling with the computer. I could hear my collection of mugs clink ominously in the locker over the diesel oven, counterpointed by a great crash from the cutlery drawer as the boat righted herself.

"Fresh breeze?" I yelled. "Are you mad? People go sailing in a fresh breeze, and there are three-foot seas out there. And this is a harbour!" The wind crescendoed fiercely to a scream, and I raised my voice in competition, holding onto the wildly rocking post by the galley with determination. "Be reasonable, my love," I coaxed at the top of my lungs, "and tell me this isn't a fresh breeze!" Another buffet of wind knocked the boat sideways. My eyes bugged out in my head.

"There may be the odd gust," John admitted. "Maybe I'll take a look at the mooring lines." He opened the companionway hatch. The sky was a dark blanket torn by screaming gusts of wind, one of which swooped into the main saloon and slapped me smartly in the face.

"Don't fall in," I yelled helpfully up the ladder. The boat trembled and the rigging shook. John was soon below again, his hair covered with a mist of salt spray.

"A bit rough out there," he said. The cutlery clanked again, and the *Inuksuk* yanked sharply on her mooring lines, then banged into the dock once more. The roaring in the rigging was deafening — like the howl of a banshee looking for souls, or the sound I make when I max out my VISA card.

There was a sudden loud crash from the deck, and we both sat bolt upright. The boom? Split rigging? We tore up the ladder carrying flashlights, to find the rubber dinghy had flipped over on the deck and bent a stanchion. The dinghy was oddly placed on the deck — crouched as if to leap with the next gust. John did not hesitate. "I'll get some rope," he said firmly. "You make sure it doesn't fly away." Spray shot over the side of the boat.

The dinghy and I looked at each other in the howling dark. It was huge and grey and rubbery and weighed even more than I did. If I threw myself on top of it and another gust came, who was I to stop it if it wanted to be free? We'd both go over. I squatted to one side of the dinghy, grabbed the painter and hoped I looked useful.

John raced back across the deck, yards of nylon line streaming behind him in the wind. Together we dragged the dinghy back into position. John looked at the tangled line. Fearlessly I plunged my hands into the writhing mass of nylon.

"Stand back, darling," I yelled over the wind. "And hold that light steady. You're looking at an Olympic-level knitter of socks." Years of expert yarn manipulation rushed to the front of my brain and I swiftly untangled the mess, handing one free end to John. Flashlights held in our teeth, we lashed the dinghy to the nearest cleats, then, bending against the wind, we staggered down the companionway. John fought with the hatch cover and closed it. "Are you still sure this is a fresh breeze?" I asked. The boat lurched wildly to port, then with another crash from the cutlery drawer, shot upright.

"Gusting to hurricane force," said John with dignity. "Let's go to bed."

I looked around the main saloon. The 110-volt lights flickered. There were books on the floor. The supper dishes crashed against each other in the sink. If I washed them and laid them out on a towel to dry, they'd all land on the floor. Besides, the apples in the hammock over the sink in the galley might strike me in the cranium as they swung viciously past. Better I should sleep lightly in the aft cabin, ready to leap out of bed at a moment's notice should my detangling skills be called upon again.

"Yes, my darling," I said. "I can enjoy this fresh breeze more from the vantage point of bed." There was a smashing sound from the locker where I keep our crystal. I ignored it. Crouched like a runner on the mark, I made myself ready to take a run at the passageway to the aft cabin. During a lull in the roaring overhead, I raced over the slanted floor next to the diesel engine, leaped into the bunk and pulled the covers over my head. I heard John fall heavily against one wall of the passageway, and he crawled into bed on his hands and knees. There was silence between us. We both listened to the screaming in the rigging. Some debris flew overhead and rattled across the deck.

"Maybe," said John, "it's a hurricane with lulls slowing to a fresh breeze."

"Darling," I said, "I believe whatever you say." At midnight we got to sleep.

Leaving Sooke

THERE WAS A small, uncomfortable-looking group of well-wishers bent against the wind and standing on the dock at Sooke Harbour. "We came to say goodbye," said one man. "Aren't you leaving?"

"My wife won't let me," said John. Behind him in the boat we could hear a snort from our crewmember, Jean-Paul.

"Thirty knots of wind! Hah! Endis will laugh at you!" A crashing wave shot over the dock and soaked the feet of our visitors. "Why, when that storm hit us in the Pacific, she didn't flinch. We ran out of food and water twice and I never heard her complain." He turned a reproachful eye on me.

"Be reasonable, Jean-Paul," I said. "There's a gale on the Strait of Juan de Fuca, a gale at Race Rocks and a gale on Haro Strait. In fact, the only place there isn't a gale is in Sooke Harbour." Another wave slopped over the feet of our visitors. They dispersed, and faint complaints floated back in snatches on the fitful wind.

"Awkward, you know ... well, people on boats ... can't count on a set departure time. *I'm* not coming back tomorrow ..."

We all trooped below and John slammed the companionway hatch against the wind. "We have to drive you back to Cowichan Bay, Jean-Paul," he said. "We'll set sail out of here in a few days."

"How sure are you of that, my love?" I asked.

"Wind's bound to let up sometime between now and spring," he said, and grinned.

I sat down with a pad and paper in a thoughtful state of mind. What were we leaving behind? Why, seals sliding silently through the tossing dark water and our pet seagull who sat vigilant and lonely by our boat every night with his chest thrust out, the mountains pale as remorse and fog as heavy as sorrow, and a community of empty powerboats. We would leave a joyful school board — after all, what could be more embarrassing than dismissing someone who wouldn't leave?

"Stop grizzling. You weren't fired," said John on his way up the companionway. "You were laid off."

"Better to starve to death in Cowichan Bay," I said melodramatically, "where all our friends are. Better to bite the bitter bullet of unemployment in a place close to our hearts — where our neighbours are all broke and love us, and their folk wisdom buoys us through times of trial. Oh, goodbye, Jean-Paul."

"Thirty knots!" Jean-Paul snorted at me. "Wussies!"

We left three days later. The water in the harbour was flat as glass, and the air was still and clear. Cautiously we motored our way out of the harbour, and with a shout Jean-Paul raised the mainsail and then the genoa. Son John Jr. and I watched nervously while John manned the wheel. Suddenly we were in the Strait of Juan de Fuca, beating into the wind. The *Inuksuk* rose to the challenge like a lady. Spray shot over the bow. There were five-foot seas and the wind filled the sails. With one rail nearly under, we shot to leeward at incredible speeds — six knots, seven knots — as the wind whipped into the sails.

"Darling," I said, "we appear to be going backwards." John pretended not to hear me.

"Darling," I said, a little louder. The boat lurched wildly and I heard a crash from below. I grabbed for a pair of binoculars sliding past me in the cockpit. "I hate to be critical," I said, "but it appears that Sooke is off our bow. There's a whole lot of the Strait of Juan de Fuca under us, and we're headed for the open sea, rear end first." Both Jean-Paul and John elaborately ignored me. I turned to John Jr.

"Son," I said, "is your old stepmother going mad, or are we headed in the wrong direction?"

John Jr. lowered his voice. "I don't think they want to talk about it." He nodded at Jean-Paul and his father. John was clutching the wheel with a determined look on his face. Jean-Paul had crawled onto the deck and was fighting with the mainsheet. The bow shot up and then sank. The dinghy floated past us on its painter, just as the genoa tore. The sheet to the genoa's roller-furling was tossing wildly forward as Jean-Paul leaped onto the deck and pulled. The genoa furled quickly into place.

"Let's get out of here," John said grimly, and put the engine into gear.

"The prop!" John Jr. yelled. "The dinghy line!" He ran flat out of words and pointed in inarticulate horror at the stern of the boat.

"Darling," I said to John, "perhaps this is the wrong time to mention this, but there appears to be a hole in the mizzen."

"Rats!" John yelled.

"Just what I thought, my darling," I said. "They chew everything. You just can't get away from them. Why are you beating your forehead on the wheel like that?"

"The prop's fouled," he moaned. "The prop's fouled and we're drifting out to sea and the genoa's torn and the mizzen has a hole in it."

"AND I'm out of a job," I said cheerfully. "Maybe prospects are better in the States. Shall I stand by the radio in case we need the coast guard? A tow? A sailmaker? Can you speak American? Are our passports in order?"

Another wave crashed over the bow. Jean-Paul and John Jr. leaned over the stern and grasped the dinghy line. John gave the controls a short shot in reverse. There was silence. Everyone froze. Jean-Paul raised his arm and gestured. Cautiously John gave the controls another shot in reverse. Spray shot up in the air off the beam of the boat. I put the binoculars down, then grabbed them again as the cockpit rocked.

"We're free!" Jean-Paul yelled. "Prop's free!"

"Yes!" John shouted.

John Jr. pulled the dinghy in and John threw the engine into gear.

"Victoria Harbour, yee haw!" I shouted, waving the binoculars over my head.

The engine throbbed and the bow cleaved strongly through the heavy seas. The dinghy, now on a short line, trailed behind us in the spray of the wake. Jean-Paul and John Jr. scrambled into the cockpit. "Thirty knots of wind out here, I think," Jean-Paul said happily.

As we chugged past the entrance to Sooke Harbour again, I climbed below to stow the binoculars. I returned more slowly and poked my head through the companionway. "My sweet," I said, "I smell smoke below."

"Rats!" John yelled, and threw the boat into neutral.

"I don't think so, darling," I said thoughtfully. "I think it's the engine. Surely even *we* couldn't melt two engines!"

Jean-Paul and John Jr. hunched in the cockpit, faces sombre, while John and I crawled towards the engine room on our hands and knees, sniffing. "I don't smell anything in the engine room," John said.

"Darling, I love you," I said, "but you are a terrible smeller." The boat rocked under our hands and knees. I leaned over the engine and sniffed. Nothing. Where was the smoke coming from? I backed out of the engine room and bumped into John.

"I can still smell smoke out here," he said. We turned our heads slowly and looked at the diesel stove. As if in a trance, I staggered over to the galley and lifted the lid of the oven. A swirl of thick black smoke curled out of the firepot, spraying soot all over the galley. I slammed the lid down and collapsed sobbing into my husband's arms.

"Oh, thank God!" I cried. "Hallelujah! The oven's shot! Praise God — it's not the engine!" Tears of relief streamed down my face. "I love you, darling. We're not on fire and we don't have to be towed. We've barely cleared Sooke Harbour, but we're doing rather well, I think — at least so far!"

"Thirty knots of wind," yelled Jean-Paul happily.

19

Part II

"WE'VE CLEARED SOOKE Harbour," I told my beloved. "It's a miracle." I was sitting in the cockpit, resplendent in a fluorescent orange cruiser suit. The wind was howling in the rigging, but our sails were furled and the bow was slicing its way through five-foot seas in the Strait of Juan de Fuca. "I think I'll go below to smell the engine," I said. I may not be a mechanic, but I know what a melting engine smells like. It smells like thousands of dollars, and the last one had nearly been the ruination of us.

We were headed for Race Rocks at six knots. We hoped to make it at slack tide.

"Darling," I said, "did the two busted sails, the fouled prop and the smoking oven get us off schedule?"

"Absolutely not," said John. "The captain who is prepared for anything never misses the tide."

"Darling," I said, "you were terribly clever to schedule an extra three hours for disasters at sea." Then I went below. The engine smelled fine. It was clean as springtime and loud as dissent. I looked complacently around the cabin. Everything that had hit the floor was unbreakable — books, navigation instruments and charts lying curled on the floor like giant wood shavings. How fortunate it was that I'd stowed the iron. Yes, we were practically experts. And we were not being towed. Tears of gratitude filled my eyes.

I climbed the companionway and looked brightly around. The

Inuksuk was rocking slightly — the seas had calmed. Through the clear air I could see the southern edge of Vancouver Island. Race Rocks lay off the starboard bow, and we made a silent passage, skating a little to port and starboard as the current swung us. It was cold. There was foam on the water like patterned lace, and the very tips of the waves crumpled into froth. There were three-foot seas. Jean-Paul, hunched over the helm, leaned forward to peer at the controls as the boat moved beneath his sturdy legs. John Jr. and his father watched ahead for logs, other boats and islands. Jean-Paul's eyesight extended to the instruments, but not beyond the bow of the boat, and the men were a little edgy. The engine throbbed steadily, and the wake behind us disappeared into dark, tossing water. "Are we there yet?" I asked.

Victoria Harbour hove into view, and there was a spirited discussion in the cockpit about how to approach. "Red right returning," I chanted sanctimoniously. All three men turned to give me a dirty look. At 1600 hours we tied up at the Fort Street government dock.

"Supper in 45 minutes," I said. "Just as soon as we've lit the diesel oven." My, but diesel ovens are slow to warm up. It was five hours later that I served dinner. Jean-Paul gave me a haggard look before he set to his meal, but John Jr. quietly tore into his food without commenting. John started to complain that the roast was underdone and the potatoes hard, but thought better of it when I offered to put his portion back in the pressure cooker to try again.

John refused to eat his carrots, then he argued for a while before bed that pickles are a vegetable (aren't they green?) and there are vitamins in vinegar, but he was weak with fatigue and his arguments lacked their usual force. Jean-Paul and John Jr., relieved they'd finally been fed, went to bed.

I lay awake for hours, rigid with terror and indigestion. I am a novice boater, but panic is something at which I excel. Would I be able to help cast off our mooring lines without falling into the sea? Would we get lost? Foul our prop again? Lose the dinghy? We couldn't ruin any more sails — we'd busted two out of three today. What if the engine failed? What if a through-hull failed? What if we hit a rock? The bilge alarm went off, and John stirred restlessly, then rolled over and started snoring. How dare John sleep when I couldn't? Everyone knows pickles aren't vegetables. When had we last changed the zincs? Five months ago? Nuts — we should have checked them. And vinegar is only good for salads and cleaning heads. And how come John's cruiser suit was a nice shade of red while I looked like a fluorescent orange popsicle in mine? The roast was only slightly underdone, after all — did I ever question John's decisions at sea? "John," I murmured gently, "do I ever argue with you?"

"Never," John said. "I'm too frightened to answer you back."

"Oh," I said, and went to sleep.

In the grey of the morning, John fired up the engine and we cast off, headed for Trial Island. Jean-Paul and John decided to hot-dog through Plumper Passage, and again past Swartz Bay, dodging ferries with our ears flattened and tails low. Lunch was sour bread and outdated luncheon meat; we really must reconsider our refrigeration system. We were still in Canada, though — there were naval ships on the horizon looming through the mist.

At 1430 we made Cape Keppel. I went below to smell the engine. John and I fell silent as we chugged past. For two years we'd broken down every time we had come to the cape. The cape was where the engine started knocking, and where the cabin filled with smoke. I looked at John. "Shall I stand by the radio?" I asked tersely. He nodded without taking his eyes away from the horizon, his mouth set.

"We're almost home," said Jean-Paul happily, "but it's getting foggy." He squinted.

I grabbed John's arm. "It's the curse," I said, my voice low and tremulous. "It's the curse of Cape Keppel."

"Be quiet," said John gently. "It's bad luck. Besides, the engine hasn't missed a beat." His voice rose a little. "I know my way home now. I laugh at fog."

"There's crab pots," I said uncertainly.

"I laugh at crab pots," said John. "We're not lost, the engine is running and we're not being towed."

My heart swelled with happiness. It was true — we were making Cowichan Bay all the way from Sooke without being towed. We hadn't radioed for help once. We hadn't collided with anything, our fire had been a piddling thing, and the engine — bless the little engine — was still running. "Are we there yet?" I asked.

"Half an hour," said John with a smile.

Nearly all of Cowichan Bay came out to greet us. I felt as loved as the returning fishers from *The Perfect Storm*. I did notice that the people running down the docks to catch our mooring lines owned the boats in the nearby slips. Not only were we loved — why, we were understood.

Home and Broke

W E WERE IN Cowichan Bay, nestled in our old spot at the end of the dock. I sighed and poked my head up the hatch. "Yes, we're home," I said to John. "Home where we're loved, and home where we fit in. Home where nobody scorns us, and home where we have been forgiven, now that we're roachless and everybody is sure we didn't import any rats from Sooke."

"It's not exactly the prosperity centre of Canada," said John, "but it's good to be back. Do we have anything for supper tonight?"

Everybody's broke in Cowichan Bay. Our neighbour and her husband, Fred, who live a few slips over, own a small business. They did so poorly last year that their accountant asked them if they would consider applying for welfare in order to raise their standard of living. I've been looking for a full-time job for three years. John Jr., who lives down the docks, hasn't been paid in six weeks, and he looks thinner every time I see him. Steve, who likes to be known by his nickname of "Screaming Liver," complains that he can barely afford beer. He's thin too, but he's awfully happy. Almost enough beer does that to a man. Only Stafford the Respectable has a job. He's a real biologist who goes to work every morning and gets weekends off and takes regular baths. But even he has not much cash. Thank goodness for John who is retired and the only person I know who isn't worried about a job. Whenever my spirits flag, he tells me another story about one of the times he was fired. This is my favourite.

Some 45 years ago, John was 17 and working as a "gardener, second class" in beautiful Coronation Gardens in London. His job was to mow the lawns. He wasn't very interested in mowing, but he was very interested in machinery, so he souped up his lawn mower to run at three times its normal speed. One day it escaped from him and mowed a bar sinister through a 150-year-old ornamental flower bed. The head gardener, beside himself with rage, called him on the carpet and told him he "wasn't fit to be a gardener, second class." He wasn't actually fired, just demoted to the tree-pruning crew where he drove around in a truck with a bunch of friendly young guys his own age who were also more interested in machinery than vegetation. Every now and then they'd prune a tree, but they tried not to let it interfere with their tea breaks. It is this, and similar inspirational stories that John tells about the triumph of the working class over management, that keeps my spirits at their optimum.

I grabbed a mug of coffee and paid a visit to Endis. She and Jean-Paul don't have any money either. "I need cheering up, Endis," I told her. "John is running out of stories about being fired and I need supper ideas. What kinds of things did you eat on your beautiful island?"

"We used to roast pigeons at home in Vanuatu," she told me shyly.

"Really?" I exclaimed, and pressed her for details. She gazed at me in some wonderment, but she was willing to explain.

"We pluck them, take out the guts, cut off the head and feet, then rub on a little soya sauce and oil, and roast them whole. We don't have wonderful spices like you do in Canada," she added humbly.

I thought about the salt, pepper and greying parsley flakes in my own galley and was too embarrassed to reply.

"And how do you catch pigeons?" I asked Endis. A pigeon fluttered past the porthole of her ketch, and I eyed it appraisingly.

"There's not so much meat on a pigeon," said Endis, "and sometimes you have to wait a long time before you trap one. We make a pigeon trap like an Indian house," she said, demonstrating with her hands.

"Tipi?" I asked.

"Yes, out of reeds, like bamboo," she said. "We pull the rope and catch the pigeon, but sometimes we catch the chicken instead. Or people shoot with a gun or bow and arrow, but people don't have that much money for guns, so mostly they shoot with a bow and arrow."

What, I wondered, would be a cheap, nutritious and easy-to-prepare meal for the cash-impaired gourmets at Cowichan Bay? I asked Endis, who was mistress of the pressure cooker.

"Beans," she said, and smiled. "Over buns, if you can afford buns."

"Then come for supper at our boat," I said, "and we will have beans. Jean-Paul likes beans, doesn't he? John is addicted to them. Then after supper we can visit and I can look at the classifieds, and John will tell us stories to cheer us up." I gave Endis a hug. "I'm glad we're back. Between you and the rest of Cowichan Bay, we're home again. We're not catching pigeons yet, but if we have to we'll know how to do it."

Chef John

"WHAT'S FOR SUPPER tonight?" I asked John, clambering down the companionway. I swung my briefcase onto the starboard settee berth and looked expectantly at my husband. On days I was offered a substitute teaching job, John was expected to man the frying pan.

"Egg and chips. And beans," John said.

"Don't like eggs. Chips are greasy. We had beans last night," I said sulkily.

"The chef gets to decide what's for dinner," John replied.

"Oh all right," I said.

I never did learn to much like eggs. As a teenager in the Arctic, I once heard the manager of the groceteria of the Hudson's Bay Company in Yellowknife (and my boss) making this extraordinary statement: "I don't know why we're getting so many complaints about the eggs. They're barely three months old and the frost hardly touched them." Many years later in Kugluktuk, Nunavut, I met a fellow high-school alumnus named Brian who told me with a laugh that his first job too was working for the Hudson's Bay Company groceteria — cracking eggs and dividing them into "edible" and "rotten" vats for the local Yellowknife restaurants.

To this day, I break eggs with distrust and suspicion. John, who can boast many more years in Canada's Arctic than I, came south with an undiminished appetite for eggs. The day I complained about being asked to fry them, John told me about the Cree women in

Great Whale River who would sit in front of their tents in summer and eat lard out of gallon tins with a teaspoon, just like ice cream.

Any Northerner worth his salt is familiar with the common navy bean. Some of us develop an immunity to its charms after a while — like the alcoholic who takes more and more of the drug with less and less effect. Others thrive on beans, and guzzle cases of them, taking as much joy in the thousandth can as they did the first time pork and beans in tomato sauce passed their lips. John is one of the latter bean-eaters. Hot beans, potatoes fried in lard and two eggs sunny side up are more attractive to my husband than "Xena, Warrior Princess." And that is saying something. John has brought his Arctic preferences south to the *Inuksuk*, including his appreciation for fine dining and determined women.

I sat in the main saloon with my knife and fork poised. "And sausages," I said, "and toast!" My enthusiasm mounted as I spotted each delectable morsel on my Corelle Livingwear plate. After all, dinner's hot, and I didn't have to cook. "Kippers — with the bones sticking up! Pickles! My favourite! Marmalade! Fried onions! Melted cheese!" I turned my loving gaze on my husband. "You're so clever, darling."

Emeril may be a world-class, food-channel chef, but he is only half as skilled as John with a slab of lard and a spatula. Sometimes you luck out and fall in love with a multi-dimensional man. John is not a TV chef, but he is an expert TV consumer who can tell by instinct where the Space Channel is, and he is master of the frying pan.

"Darling," I said, pushing back my plate, "I'd do the dishes tonight, but I know you're better at it than I am. And since I didn't have to cook, let me run out to Cowichan Foods to get you some replacement beans. And eggs. Tomorrow you can fry me up some 'gourmet surprise.'"

Bored Onboard

"Good morning, darling," I said.

"The name is Dook, John Dook. I'll have my coffee stirred, not shaken," my husband replied.

"Oh, for goodness' sake, John," I said. "No more James Bond novels for you. You're far too sensitive to read them."

"What's that, Moneypenny?" he said.

"You need a hobby," I said.

"How about home dentistry?" asked John. "I already own a grinder. Think of the money we'll save. I could do wonders with a piece of string and a doorknob."

"We don't own any doorknobs," I said, "and I'm not letting you anywhere near my teeth, especially with boat tools."

John was getting bored. Nothing at all had broken down onboard the *Inuksuk* for at least a month. After the first few years of living aboard you can identify the mechanical breakdowns. It's sort of like being beaten up by someone you know. We had become excitement junkies, nerves readied for the next disaster. We prided ourselves on rising to the occasion.

There was the time we turned one valve the wrong way and a resounding "ping" rang through the air, followed by the sound of rushing water as one of our steel water tanks gave way. We remained calm and donated generously to the local welder. We have since become expert at filling the tanks — turn the left valve right and the right valve left, open the fourth red valve and close the other three — or is it turn the left valve left and the right valve right? The instructions are posted on the bulkhead.

Then there was the time the diesel oven died in the middle of winter. It gave a little hiccup and expired. The corpse winked at us reproachfully, as if resentful that we were unable to save it, but we didn't even hesitate. Right away we hired someone to revive it.

The electric head once gave up on us, and I remained in complete control of my senses. "Fix it, darling," I said, and John paid a small fortune for parts, closed the seacocks and dove in up to his elbows.

When the battery charger blew up and all our batteries went flat we didn't miss a beat; we bought a new battery charger.

Another time the oven fan creaked to a halt. We were getting used to disaster by this time, so with calm confidence we paid for a new fan.

The day the plastic water pipes burst, John knew exactly where to buy compatible hose and new fittings, and by the time the bilge pump gave out and the floorboard screws were stripped, we got a preferred-customer discount.

Now that everything has broken down once, we're prepared for any eventuality. We prowled restlessly through the boat, testing the bilge alarm, examining the dials on the battery charger and peering into the firepot to see if it needed cleaning. We ran the head a time or two to see if the macerator was functioning. We flipped the 12-volt lights to see if we needed bulbs. Nothing. We looked at each other.

"Want to rent a movie?" I asked.

"No," John replied. "I've seen them all."

"Want to watch TV?"

"No, there's nothing on."

"What do you want to do?" I asked.

"I want to put fillings in your teeth, but you won't let me," he said.

Older-than-Dirt Don, who lives nearby on an impossibly small trimaran, knocked excitedly on the boat. "Hey, folks," he yelled. "Your tarp's in the water, your stern line is working loose and they're predicting a bad blow later. They're saying tonight's the night the docks break up."

I looked over at John. There was a look of blissful happiness on his face.

"We're back to normal," he said. I'm sure the sigh he gave was one of pure contentment.

Be Prepared

"Darling," I said, "what's up with the trip this summer?"

"It's on," said John. "Just as soon as we buy the last of the equipment."

"We have equipment coming out of our ears," I complained. "We have electronic equipment, radio equipment, mechanical equipment, lines, tackle and charts. All we need is a few spares, say, 300 feet of line and parts for the engine — impellers, hoses, clamps, engine oil to specifications, 30 or 40 nuts, bolts, o-rings, filters, a fuel injector pump or two and a few tools."

"I never should have let you take that diesel engine course," John said. "You've become a most annoying armchair expert."

"I may not be able to tell the head from the oil pan, darling," I said, "but my theoretical knowledge is above reproach, and my nagging is prime. What a team we make!" John snorted. "Everyone knows men don't 'do' preventive maintenance. And call me suspicious, but your daughter Lisa has told me stories about 'Vacations I've taken with Daddy' that fill my heart with fear. The tire bounding down the Mackenzie Highway in front of the car, and the time the hood flew off and nailed the top of the car on its way past. And do you remember when the windshield wipers gave out and your first wife, Louise, had 700 miles of gravel highway to drive, with five kids and no rest stops in the pouring rain? She made all the kids take off their shoelaces, and attached them to a windshield wiper, and for 700 miles the kids pulled

32

back and forth — whup, whap, whup, whap. Your first wife was a saint."

"The Mackenzie Highway was tough on cars," John admitted.

"And the Pacific Ocean is tough on boats," I said, "but a few spares will solve the problem. Also, some through-hull plugs, fittings, a sack of cement for repairs, rebar, some sailcloth, a spare stanchion, bolts and Plexiglas, and we'll need a couple of pounds of screws and some spare rigging. Do you think everything will fit in the forward cabin?"

"A sack of cement? What do you plan to do to the boat?" John asked. "There's not enough room onboard for all that stuff."

"Of course there is, darling," I said, "and a few tools, a cement saw, a power drill, a bolt cutter, wrenches to fit every bolt on the engine, hand tools — you never know — and don't forget extra propane, diesel fuel, teak oil, lamp oil and some alcohol in case we decide to buy an alcohol stove."

"You sank the boat about three paragraphs ago," said John. "Will there be room for provisions?"

"A barrel of flour and a few tin cans, darling. We'll need spare can openers, extra cutlery, maybe a fishhook or two, some tackle, a canner and a few jars — it'll be berry season — lids for the jars, some unbreakable dishes, extra tin mugs and a rice steamer, deep fryer, breadmaker, generator with spare parts and jugs filled with water and fuel — we can fit them in the head."

"We're not going offshore," John said. "We're going part way up the Inside Passage."

"And we need to be prepared, darling," I said. "Who shall we take as crew?"

"There's no room left for crew," John said. "You're trying to fill the boat with junk."

"Junk!" I gasped. "You're calling my 300 books and spare parts junk?"

"Three hundred books!" John exclaimed, "We can't take 300 books!"

"Of course we can, darling," I said. "We'll need something to read during those lingering twilights when we're at anchor. How many anchors do we have?"

"Two," said John.

"Only two?" I asked.

"Now stop right there," said John. "All we need is an EPIRB and some repairs to the dinghy. Then we'll be ready to go."

"And a repair kit for the dinghy," I said. "Spare patch material, glue, a knife, an extra foot pump and extra line. Do they sell spare parts for EPIRBs? Well, maybe we can get two of them. Do we have parts for the outboard? We'll need some. And spare oars, an extra couple of oarlocks and plywood to make repairs to the seat. I don't plan to get caught unprepared. But there's one item I absolutely won't go anywhere without."

"What's that?" John asked.

"Ten shoelaces, darling. You never know when they'll come in handy."

Beyond the Dock

Aʟʟ ᴡᴀs ᴄᴀʟᴍ at Cowichan Bay. The early-morning sun beamed down on the weathered docks, resplendent with telephone wires and TV cables, hoses for water with a fine spray coming out of the holes, and a venerable Siamese cat picking his desultory way over the planking. Nika, the pit bull onboard the powerboat *Shogun*, opened one eye, then decided to let the cat pass unchallenged. The cat rolled once in a warm patch of sunlight, then sprang gracefully onto the wooden box abeam of the *Inuksuk* and sat still, nose inquisitive and tail flicking lightly at the very tip.

I poked my head up through the companionway. "Hullo, Buddy," I said. "Mommy throw you out again?" The cat meowed once, then jumped for the cockpit and collapsed in a furry ecstasy of purring in front of me. I reached over the doorway to tickle his jaw. "You're a lucky kitty, you know," I said. "The cat before you got sent to the pound when he was a bad kitty." I glanced at my neighbour's newly scrubbed floor mats, hung out to dry over the boom. "It's not just you, though," I continued. "It's all your little neighbourhood kitty friends — the ones with glands." Buddy meowed and pushed his head into my hand. "Mommy's children burst into pathetic sobs at bedtime, so Daddy Fred went back to the pound to reclaim the cat, and Mommy said her children were not friendly for a while and even though the cat was reinstated as a family member in good standing, Mommy's name was mud. And she'd never sprayed furniture in her life. She didn't think that was fair at all." I paused for breath. "So watch your step. And no, you can't eat breakfast with us."

Buddy flicked his tail and gave me a disconcerted look, head cocked to one side. Then he stalked majestically to the side of the boat and leaped down, pausing to give me an offended glance before he walked purposefully down the dock.

"Beware, Buddy," I called after him. "Beware the woman going through menopause. We're like triffids. There are more of us than you think." Buddy ignored me, but I heard a shout from the boat with the laundry.

"Hullo!"

"Hullo to you, too," I called back. "Want coffee?"

My neighbour climbed aboard. "Has my cat been annoying you?" she asked.

"Buddy doesn't annoy us," I said. "He just uses our boat as a flophouse now and then."

"Well, he annoys me," she said grimly. "Fred adores that cat, but the attraction escapes me. Do you know the number of the pound?"

"Now calm yourself," I said. "Buddy loves you."

"I'm not in love with Buddy," she said. "I've cleaned my last carpet of cat spray."

"It wasn't even Buddy," I said reasonably. "It's usually Buddy's little buddies."

"Three or four of them, judging by the mess," she said. "If I can't dispose of Buddy, can I at least get rid of Fred? Does the pound take husbands?" She laughed and took a sip of coffee. "Enough about that. Are you ready for your trip? Do YOU take husbands?"

"Only my own this time," I said.

She put down her coffee cup. "So who's your crew?" she asked.

"Me," I said.

"Hmmmmm," she said. "Do you have my cell phone number?"

"Of course," I said. "Yours and everyone else in Cowichan Bay who might be persuaded to perform a rescue at sea. We haven't been towed for a couple of years — not since Al and Loreena came out in the middle of the night in *Running Free*, but you never know. Just in case it takes a while for our neighbours to get to us, I've stowed enough provisions and equipment to rescue the Franklin Expedition. Every time I feel nervous about the trip, I go out and buy another 16 rolls of toilet paper or a case of beans. Or a kilo of pancake mix and a half-dozen bottles of liquid detergent. We may be a little overstocked on some items. Want more sugar in your coffee? We have 20 kilos onboard. Or do you want to have breakfast with us? We have enough oatmeal to swell up and sink the boat. Toast? I have a gallon of margarine. Another cup of coffee? We have 30 kilos stored in the locker over the propane stove. I had to pitch most of our dishes to fit in the ten packages of cookies, the $60 worth of fishing lures and the three economy-sized bottles of lemon juice. Scurvy, you know." I clutched my mug. "What if we go places where they don't accept VISA? I may be in over my head."

"Now, now," said my neighbour. "I'm sure you'll do fine. Want a ship's cat?"

"There's no place to put one," I said. "We're storing three boxes of charts, a sextant and two survival suits in the forward cabin. We have extra water jugs lashed to the railings, and tools and spare parts crammed into the lockers. I wanted to store soda pop in the bilge, but John said anything that had been in our bilge would never touch his lips. Pretty fastidious for a man who said all we'd need in the way of provisions would be beans and some weevilly biscuit. He'll be glad of my five kilos of raisins and ten litres of grape juice when we're gone. Every time John bought a spare part, I nagged until he bought two or three more. I had him almost talked into a 20-gallon drum of hydraulic oil, but he put his foot down."

"A ship's cat comes in handy," said my neighbour. "They chase rats."

"Why, we haven't had rats on the docks since Sooke," I laughed.

"Buddy just loves to chase bugs," said my neighbour. "How are your roaches?"

"Gone for ages," I said smugly. "That nice young exterminator got the last two. We figure they cost us $125 per roach. I wonder if I can fit another 16 rolls of toilet paper in the head, and some spare flashlight batteries? I feel ready for anything."

"Except those lonely nights at anchor," said my neighbour. "Buddy is awfully good company."

I began to realize we were talking at cross purposes. "Are you trying to get rid of your cat?" I asked, putting down my coffee cup.

"Oh, not exactly," she said evasively. "I'm just trying to offer a little neighbourly assistance. I'll throw in Fred too if you like — no extra charge. He's a pretty good sailor and he doesn't get as seasick as Buddy."

"It's a tempting offer," I said, "but John really does want us to go by ourselves. He thinks it's time I gained confidence and skill. I've improved a lot since the time I got us lost on the way home from Ganges — but why rehash old history? Want more coffee?"

"No thanks," she said genially, then put her cup down. "You know, if I can't give you my cat or my husband, let me give you my very best wishes for a safe trip. And some advice. There are two ways to deal with disaster at sea. One is to burst into tears. The other is to bite your tongue and try to enjoy yourself."

"I'll try to remember that," I said humbly.

We hugged each other as she left. "You'll do well, I know," she said.

Buddy meandered back down the dock and meowed questioningly at me. "Go home, Buddy," I said, "and embrace your fate. There are two ways to deal with domestic disaster. One is to run away. The other is to face your fear. I wonder if I can get a deal on toilet paper before tomorrow?"

Clam Bay Bound

WHEN WE PUSHED off I had a song on my lips:
"No more pencils, no more books,
No more principals' dirty looks."
Ah, the life of the substitute teacher! The time the principal lost his balance and slipped in the oats, peas and beans strewn all over the kindergarten floor — well, that could hardly be called my fault. And later that afternoon when an irate parent phoned to complain I'd told her tot that his teacher was dying — well, that wasn't exactly what I'd said. I added that principal's name to the list of administrators who think I'm an idiot. His jaw was rigid. And that riot in the junior-high library? Could've happened to anyone. Or the time I left a school with the vice-principal's keys — the memories slid past like foamy water as we slipped out of our slip. Jean-Paul held our stern line as we swung heavily around the corner, then flung it to me with a fluid throw. "Goodbye, goodbye," we called, "goodbye."

Two minutes later at the fuel dock, Jean-Paul was there to catch our lines. I leaned toward John.

"Does he want to be sure we go?" I asked. "Or is he just nervous we won't make it?" I glanced furtively over one shoulder. "*I'm* nervous we won't make it. Is this the wrong time to tell you I think we're going to die?"

"Of course we're going to die," John said, "but probably not on this trip." I briefly weighed substitute teaching against an uncertain future at sea and decided to take my chances with the ocean. No longer the ignored nonentity in the staff room — onboard the *Inuksuk* I was a valuable member of the crew.

The day before, we'd bought another length of anchor chain, and hadn't my eagle eye spotted the salesman's blatant attempt to cheat us? And hadn't I called him to task for it, at which point he was so annoyed he overcharged us by about 20 percent plus tax? But John was so anxious to load the shiny links of chain into the trunk of the car that we paid hugely without a murmur. We felt guilty giving so much money to a marine store that wasn't our usual outfitter. "That'll teach you," I told my husband. But John still had a glaze over his eyes caused by the reflected glare of the chain and he didn't hear me. Buying boat parts puts John into a kind of trance, and he needs to be protected from himself. Still, at the Power Squadron course they said you need lots of chain.

"Goodbye, goodbye," we called to Jean-Paul, "goodbye."

The diesel engine throbbed strongly — so strongly we missed *Shogun* by a good three feet as we pulled away from the fuel dock. "Your fenders!" yelled Jean-Paul from the fuel dock. "Pull up your fenders!"

Busily coiling up the stern line, I pretended that pulling up the fenders had been my plan all along.

We were headed for Clam Bay on Thetis Island where we planned to anchor that night. A shudder ran through my psyche. Just thinking about the coming ordeal gave me the chills. "It may be," I told John, "that I am the weakest link in the anchor chain."

"Nonsense," said John. We motored heavily around Separation Point, as ponderously as a rock swung at the end of a string. Then we dodged logs floating lazy as crocodiles in the water. As we headed toward Thetis Island, I was reassured by the sight of the village of Crofton spilling into the bay, and the Saltspring ferry chugging from port to starboard across our bow. My eyes followed the sturdy craft longingly. I bet the people onboard the ferry didn't have to choose between substitute teaching and death.

"Don't be silly," said John. "We're just going to anchor. Which one is Kuper Island?"

"Let me look at the chart," I said. "That looks like Tent Island ahead. Give me the binoculars. What direction are we bearing? Heaven spare us! There are rocks all through here. Whose idea was this anyway?"

"Now calm down," said John. "According to this chart, the rocks are all under enough water that we're safe."

"It's an old chart," I said darkly. "And at the Power Squadron course, they said you're not supposed to use old charts."

"Rocks don't reproduce," John said firmly.

"How do you know? I bet they do." I said, but weakly. "It's time to put a life jacket on. I'm going forward to look for rocks."

"Fine," said John.

I didn't see any rocks at all, but I directed John around one or two stalks of seaweed just to enhance my credibility. My, but I felt important. As we wended our way into Clam Bay I fell to my knees. "Land!" I exclaimed. "Land ho, darling. We've escaped death again!"

"We've been within sight of land since we started," John pointed out.

We motored slowly into the encircling arms of the bay. Two sleek sailboats lay at anchor, their rode straight down in the placid water. We anchored in 40 feet of water but I let out 60 feet of chain, then another 100, just to be sure. We slowly backed into the rocks while anchor chain shot gaily out the bow of the boat at a great pace.

"Tighten the winch!" John yelled. "For heaven's sake, tighten the anchor winch! We're losing all our chain!"

"What?" I yelled back. "Which is the anchor winch? Oh, THAT anchor winch!" The boat stopped, and John slowly recovered from his cardiovascular event.

"Darling," I said gently, "at the Power Squadron course, they said you had to have an anchor-rode-to-depth ratio of 7:1. Since we're in 40 feet of water, according to my calculations we should let out 280 feet of anchor rode. At least. Maybe more."

John was gasping slightly and hanging onto the wheel of the boat. He opened his eyes and looked at me. "Ever since that Power Squadron course ..." he began.

"I've become an even more invaluable member of the crew?" I said.

"Exactly my point," John said, changing tack in a hurry. "You did very well. But we only have 200 feet of anchor chain in total."

"What?" I said.

"And not all of it has been tested in our winch," he continued.

"What?" I said.

"So perhaps we should be satisfied with *most* of our chain for now."

"What?" I said.

I slept uneasily. I woke John up twice to ask him if he thought he should get out of bed to check the anchor. He didn't think so. "There isn't a ripple on the water," he said, so I fell back asleep.

In the morning we had a delicious, nervous breakfast of bread toasted over a propane flame. John fired up the engine and I positioned myself over the manual anchor winch, ready for anything. I heaved and grunted for a while, pulling in yards and yards of chain, but when I got to the last 75 feet, there was trouble. For every six inches I pulled in, the brand-new chain slipped back three. I was horrified. John hurried to the bow of the boat and helped me winch. The new chain looked like an exact fit, but it was ever so slightly too large.

"At the Power Squadron course," I said, "they told us you are supposed to test all your equipment before you leave." There was no response from John, who struggled harder with the winch handle. He began to gasp slightly.

"At the Power Squadron course," I said, "they told us your anchor chain has to fit your winch."

John began to force the chain directly into the hold, throwing his body straight back as he clutched the chain. His face was strained and intent, and the veins on his neck started to swell.

"At the Power Squadron course," I said, "they told us you have to

42

know your equipment."

"Perhaps," John said mildly, "you could pull for a while." So I did. With great heaves, I fought and struggled. Suddenly the anchor was clear of the water. Working in tandem, John and I put the anchor in place, then quietly, stealthily, we slunk out of Clam Bay.

I resolved to be silent, and as subtle as only a graduate of a Power Squadron course can be. I resolved to be as profound in my quiet as a substitute teacher in an alien staff room, and as wise and wordless as a resident of Cowichan Bay caught doing something dumb.

"Goodbye, goodbye," I said to Clam Bay, "goodbye."

Date with Destiny

"Dodds Narrows," I moaned. "Do we have to go through Dodds Narrows? Couldn't we go around them?"

"Where's the fun in that?" John asked.

Dodds Narrows loomed large in my brain, my brain which was shrivelled with terror. A straight run north to Nanaimo led smack through the narrows; a detour would take up to three hours through rock-infested waters. Slack tide at Dodds Narrows was at 11:05 AM and there was a 15-minute window. At other times, the foaming water rushed through at speeds up to nine knots. The jagged opening would admit one boat at a time, which would hasten through with the bow tossing and the eyes of the captain and crew rolling wildly. The prospect of churning water made my breakfast lie uneasily on my stomach. I was prepared not to enjoy the coming ordeal. The engine sounded as busy as a hive of bees and the *Inuksuk* ploughed through the water sturdily, heavily, inexorably toward Dodds Narrows.

"What time is it?" I asked John. "Exactly."

"Ten thirty-two," John replied.

"Thirty-three minutes until death," I said.

"You have the wrong attitude," John said. "There's maybe four inches of chop, the sun is bright and the engine hasn't missed a beat. The breeze is soft, and the water is sliding gently past the hull. What's your beef?"

"My beef? My beef? Surely the condemned is allowed to complain a little before the execution." John snorted and turned back to the wheel. "I'll try to snuffle quietly," I said. "Just ignore me. I'll be practically silent. I know my place, and it's that of the quiet one in the cockpit. What time is it? Exactly."

"Ten thirty-five," John said.

"Thirty minutes until death," I said. "Why couldn't Nanaimo be more conveniently located — say on *this* side of Dodds Narrows? Why is it my destiny to go adventuring with you when what I really want is calm, quiet waters at a sturdy dock and perhaps a purring cat to keep me company? We should have brought Buddy — the neighbour's cat — and Fred — the neighbour. And Jean-Paul — he's been offshore. What time is it?"

"Ten forty-one," John said.

"Twenty-four minutes until death," I said. "Why are you slowing down? What's wrong?" The engine purled back and the boat slowed.

"We're almost there," John said. "We'll have to wait in line."

To starboard and port of us was a line of gleaming white powerboats, all steadily working their way past us. The captains at the wheels all had straining necks, grim faces and popping eyes in common, I noticed, and nobody stopped to wave.

"What time is it?" I asked.

"Ten fifty-two," John replied.

"Thirteen minutes until death," I said.

"I really wish you'd stop saying that," John said.

At the entrance to the narrows a small cluster of powerboats sat in a ragged line. We took our place well back. Occasionally a boat would shoot through the passage toward us and pop out our end like a cork flying out of a bottle. The boat would churn past us with the crew waving, smiling and rejoicing, the swine.

One by one the boats ahead of us slipped through the opening. I could smell their fear. An aluminum commercial fishing boat as big as a mountain ploughed past us and disappeared determinedly into the narrow entrance. Suddenly it was our turn. The water moved beneath the boat as if a giant Mixmaster was stirring it. John's jaw was set. "It's only eleven o'clock!" I yelled. "We've got five minutes until slack tide. We're too early. We're not supposed to die for another five minutes!"

"Fifteen-minute window," John yelled back, and swung the wheel wildly as the bow strained to port.

Too frightened to close my eyes, I concentrated on a steep outcrop to starboard. The *Inuksuk* was inching her way past it. The engine throbbed, and the bow was tossed from port to starboard. John, looking exhilarated and even happy, fought with the wheel. A frightened-looking crew in a white powerboat on the opposite side of the narrows watched our uncertain progress with trepidation. As the seconds slipped by, the waters seemed to diminish in strength and didn't fight us as hard; they appeared to thrash in muddied disarray. Our little purchase increased, and the smooth rocks slid past almost quickly. I began to gasp with relief. "What time is it?" I asked. "Exactly."

"Eleven-oh-five and we're through," John said happily. I sagged into the cockpit, overcome with relief.

"Is it a girl or a boy?" I asked weakly.

"I'm the one who did all the work," said John. The powerboat with the worried-looking crew entered the passage and I grinned and waved, getting a weak smile from the captain in return.

"That poor man," I said compassionately. "He looks almost sick with fear." I waved encouragingly at him and gave him the thumbs up. "Well, some people just aren't courageous about these things. If you get to the narrows at slack tide, they're really a piece of cake. Coffee, darling?"

Quo Vadis?

Nanaimo was a dream of happiness. We were nestled comfortably at a dock so luxurious I felt rich just stepping on it. The sun shone warmly and a gentle breeze ruffled our raggedy Canadian flag. "What time did the marine mechanic say he'd be here?" I asked my husband. I stretched my arms and, arching my back, I leaned more comfortably against the backrest in the cockpit.

"Early tomorrow morning," John said unhappily. While we were docking, our prop shaft had come out of the coupling, so we were paying huge amounts of money to stay at the marina. This was the third time our coupling had failed us in a dozen dockings, and John was not heartened. By contrast, I felt quite cheerful. Putting oneself into the hands of a marine mechanic is as soothing as going to the hairdresser. He reassures you, pampers you and tells you exactly the lies you want to hear. I was prepared to luxuriate in the experience.

"Want to go shopping, darling?" I asked. "Everything we can imagine is at the mall. Even the Internet, if we drop enough twoonies into the machine."

"No," said John.

"Want a shower? There's tons of fresh water here."

"Nope," said John.

"Shall I play you a CD? There's electricity."

"No thanks," said John.

"Cheer up, darling," I said. "Maybe this mechanic will solve our problem. Want coffee? Propane's cheap here."

"Want a coupling," John said sulkily. "Want a coupling that works."

Our new mechanic was unctuous and friendly, and he threw the coupling together with hardly any effort. It occurred to me that the prop shaft that slides in easily slides out easily as well, but I suppressed the thought as being unworthy of me. We paid gladly and reversed out of our slip with reckless abandon, headed northeast across Georgia Strait for Secret Cove.

Secret Cove was nestled on the mainland, north of Vancouver. Between us and Secret Cove lay the daunting mass of Georgia Strait, which looked large and unfriendly even on our little chart. We had put all our waypoints into the GPS, and I was proud of the straight lines I'd drawn through Rainbow Channel, just east of Nanaimo, and across Whiskey Golf — so named for the giant "WG" on the chart. Our course lay first through Rainbow Channel. Then we'd nip across Whiskey Golf, tackle Georgia Strait with grace and élan and sail into Secret Cove triumphantly in time for dinner. But there was a 20-knot wind on our nose.

"Can't sail today," John said glumly. The seas were six to eight feet but the *Inuksuk* rode them with ease. Spray shot over the bow, and then a wave washed the foredeck. We slowly made our way through Rainbow Channel, fighting a two-knot current. We were able to manage only three knots. Nearly relaxed, or at least not panicked enough to start screaming and throw myself overboard, I served coffee and a handful of trail mix. I looked behind us.

"Darling," I said, "there's a most peculiar boat racing up on our port side. It looks like a giant bathtub with police lights on top. Are there pirates in Whiskey Golf? With military haircuts?"

"I don't think so," said John. The boat pulled up alongside and John got on the radio.

"Range Patrol vessel?" John repeated. "Oh my goodness." He handed me the radio.

"What's wrong?" I asked.

"Oh, nothing much, really," John said, swinging the bow to port. "We're in a torpedo firing range. The Range Patrol wants us to leave these waters because they're firing torpedoes."

I gasped out loud and raced for the chart. My tracking line led smack through the middle of an area marked ... I squinted to see better ... "see warning." I looked it up. "Armed forces equipment tests are frequently conducted ..."

"Oh dear," I said, embarrassed. "I suppose I should have noticed it while I was plotting our course." The friendly-looking Range Patroller waved us toward Winchelsea Island, then tore off at an incredible speed. I watched him disappear, his police lights zipping around the top of the dodger of his boat.

We bore 90 degrees to port for an hour, and the Range Patrol boat reappeared like a good angel to tell us we could proceed northeast to Secret Cove. "By the way, you've lost your dinghy!" he yelled through his window. Our heads snapped aft. Trailing in the water was a thin yellow dinghy painter with a bow line knot bouncing through the five-foot chop. The dinghy was missing.

"Lord save us," I moaned. "Our little dinghy is gone forever, lost and wandering among torpedoes."

"I was shot at once by German border guards," John said thoughtfully, "but I've never been torpedoed before."

"Oh stop it, darling," I begged. "Can we go home?"

"Nonsense," said John. "We're halfway there. We can't let a little thing like a lost dinghy stop us." Grimly we proceeded across Georgia Strait. I went below in a collapsed state to recover from the loss of our dinghy — our special little dinghy I'd spent so many hours rowing around Cowichan Bay. Our special little dinghy I'd saved from a hurricane in Sooke. I poked my head up the companionway.

"My love," I said, "the whole cabin smells of diesel."

"Take the wheel," John said and shot below.

The boat was being beaten by the tide, and the wind was on our nose. I braced myself in the cockpit. Salt spray rained upon me. The

Inuksuk swung from side to side, fighting the tide. John's pale face appeared at the companionway entrance. "We have a bad diesel leak from the engine," he said. "We'll have to turn it off."

"Saints preserve us," I moaned.

"Hold the flashlight for me," said John, "and I'll try to repair it."

"Heaven spare us," I said. I crawled below and looked in the engine room. At the end of my flashlight beam was a three-foot spray of diesel fuel. "God be with us," I exclaimed.

John turned off the engine. All that could be heard was the slapping of the waves under the hull, the moaning of the wind in the rigging, the sharp tapping of the halyards and my ragged breathing, which had suddenly become louder.

John fiddled in the rocking engine room. "Can't fix it," he said, "and the wind has died. We can't even sail. We'll have to turn the engine back on and hope for the best."

The engine roared to life and the *Inuksuk* turned heavily back on course. I clambered into the cockpit with trembling legs, my New Testament clutched in a whitened fist. "If it's all the same to you, darling," I said, "I think I'll read the Bible for a while. Leave nothing to chance, I always say." Determinedly, I began at Matthew.

An hour later, I had finished Acts and I felt heartened and happy. I looked up from my Bible. The sun shone brightly in the cockpit and the waves had calmed. "Listen to this, darling," I said excitedly. "Paul of Tarsus had an even worse voyage than ours. They set out in hurricane season. Storm-tossed and frightened, the crew threw the cargo, the tackle and then the provisions overboard. The ship ran aground near the island of Malta, and the stern was beaten to pieces by the surf. The passengers and crew had to swim for shore, clutching pieces of the boat. And not a soul was lost," I finished triumphantly. "Put your hand in the hand of the Man who stills the waters."

"And this story has cheered you up?" John asked.

"Absolutely, darling," I said. "We are not the only sailors who have run straight into disaster. Two thousand years ago Murphy was alive and functioning, and only the prayers of Saint Paul could prevent the deaths of the terrified crew. My theology may be a little mixed, but I think I'm getting a handle on this. Next trip out, let's take a member of the clergy with us. I wonder if any of the clergy I know like sailboats?"

John ignored me. "Take these binoculars," he said, "and see if you can find Secret Cove."

"I bet there's a marine mechanic there, darling." I said. "Maybe he'll solve our problems. After this, quo vadis?"

"We are going to Nanaimo," said John. The sun shone on his head like a halo. "We will go back to Nanaimo."

Coupling Problems

As we approached Secret Cove, I leaned out the starboard side of the *Inuksuk* with the binoculars. My cruiser suit was encrusted with salt spray and I was droopy-eyed with fatigue. The water was calm — we were in the lee of Texada Island, and powerboats were scattered on the water like pearls. "We're somewhere near people," I said hopefully. "So Secret Cove is somewhere around here." A powerboat motoring along the shore slipped out of view, and I strained my eyes. "That must be the cove," I said. I focussed the binoculars. "There — red triangle — we enter to port of that channel marker. Aren't I clever, darling?"

"Of course you are, my little dumpling," said John diplomatically, maintaining silence about the hysterical outbursts, panic attacks and uncontrolled sobbing in which I'd indulged while crossing Georgia Strait. Cautiously we motored closer. A small gap appeared in the coastline. I was quite at my ease now that I was fairly sure we weren't going to sink, go adrift or die by torpedo strike. With complacency I admired the channel marker as we chugged past. We hugged the tiny island in the entrance and swung to port, gaily waving at the fuel dock staff who enthusiastically waved back at us.

"Not here!" they yelled. "Over there. Over there." John obligingly threw the engine into reverse, and suddenly, our journey was at an end. We hung silently in the water, our prop shaft swinging free of our coupling — free as a salmon swimming upstream — free as a gull wheeling overhead — free as ...

"John, darling, ungrit your teeth and tell me how we're going to dock without a prop." We were six feet out from the fuel dock, and the attractive young woman there looked confused.

"Aren't you coming in?" she asked politely, perhaps thinking from our fierce expressions that we had taken a sudden dislike to her immaculate fuel dock.

"We've lost our coupling," I said. "Can you catch lines?" I threw a spring line at her. Despair gave me strength, and I nearly hit her on the head. When it became obvious that we were engineless and without power, the marina staff dragged us off to one side underneath their upscale restaurant.

That evening we could hear the happy sounds of carefree diners noshing on spotted prawns with brandy sauce à la Secret Cove. We treated the diners to the aromatic delights of onions and canned ham fried in margarine. Less than 12 hours later the owner of the marina himself escorted us to an obscure corner away from the shiny tourist boats and into a realm that could best be described as "funky."

"I told you we should have painted the boat this year," I told my husband. I looked at him. "Why so glum, darling?"

"I wanted this to be a fun vacation for you, and everything has gone wrong," he said. "Now we're broken down again and we're stuck in Secret Cove."

"Oh no, darling," I said. "This has been a wonderful vacation. Every time we set out I think we're going to die, so when we don't it's a pleasant surprise. Why, I took the wheel at least three times, and I hauled anchor at Clam Bay without falling overboard. When we lost our coupling in Nanaimo, didn't I have the presence of mind to yell for help? I was paralyzed with fear crossing Georgia Strait just on general principles, but I didn't actually break down until the encounter with the Range Patrol, who were ticked that we tried to cross a torpedo testing range. And didn't I hold the flashlight steady so we could see the three-foot spray of diesel from the broken fitting shoot across the engine room? And we made it all the way to Secret Cove before we broke down again. This is a record for us. We weren't even towed. We were never in any actual danger, except for the torpedoes, and here we are — tied up at a nice dock and still alive. I'm having a really good time, darling. You plan the best vacations!"

The Secret of Secret Cove

"SECRET COVE IS so secret," I told John. "Nobody knows we're here and we don't know anybody. I think I'll go for a walk down the dock and see if I can catch a glimpse of our marine mechanic. He said not to phone him, but I'd like to at least look at him. What was it he said again when he looked at our coupling?"

"He said, 'What the heck is this,'" said John.

"Yes, that's it," I said. "That's what he said all right. And what else did he say?"

"He said, 'Who installed this piece of junk?'" said John.

"Do you know what this means, darling?" I lowered my voice.

"No, what?" said John.

"It means that hidden away in Secret Cove all this time was the mechanic who is actually going to solve our coupling problems. Forever." Reverently I fondled the coupling, now sitting on the settee berth. "'What the heck is this? Who installed this piece of junk?' I want to look at the man who said those words."

"Be patient," said John. "He said he'd be back in a few days. Don't frighten him away."

"Now then, darling," I said, "He's not a species of rare bird."

"It's worse than that," said John. "He's a marine mechanic. Marine mechanics are rare, they may be temperamental and we're completely at their mercy — he's more like a white leopard or a Siberian tiger."

"I want to see one up close," I said.

"You mean a white leopard or a Siberian tiger?" John asked.

"No. A marine mechanic. The marine mechanic of Secret Cove."

"Just don't frighten him off," said John again. "Let's stay quietly here and see if he'll approach us."

"He said after Friday he was going on a three-day holiday," I said. "I don't think I can wait until next Tuesday before I see him."

"Our neighbours at the dock have offered to drive us into Sechelt to shop," said John. "Want to go?"

"What if we miss him?" I said. "I don't think we can risk it. You can buy CDs and ice cream anytime, but it isn't every day you get a glimpse of a marine mechanic. No, darling, I know what my priorities are. If I can't spot him, can I make one little phone call? Please?"

"Absolutely not," said John. "He specifically stated we were not to phone him."

"Then I'll phone my neighbour in Cowichan Bay instead," I said.

The sky was blue — as achingly blue and shiny as a jewel, and cirrus clouds were etched against the sky. "It's going to rain," John said sagely. "I can tell by the clouds."

"Darling," I said, "the last time you said that was in Kugluktuk, Nunavut, and it rained a week later in Yellowknife, a thousand miles away."

"It rained, didn't it?" said John. "Go make your call."

I walked sedately down the dock. Using my VISA card, I dialled on the pay phone next to the fuel dock, and my neighbour's cheerful voice came on the line.

"Oh, Catherine!" she exclaimed. "Where are you? Do you need a tow?"

"Well, not yet," I said. "We're broken down in Secret Cove. Our coupling is not the right coupling and our marine mechanic is having a new one made up for us in Vancouver. I'd tell you what he charges an hour, but I know you have a weak heart. We haven't seen him in three days and the marina charges over $200 a week — plus tax. We figure we'll be here a couple of weeks at least, so alert Al and Loreena of *Running Free* — the marina may cut our lines when we're completely drained of money, and we may need a tow then. This is going to cost us thousands."

There was a pause on the line. "I lost 65 cents in the accounting books today," she said, "but I feel better now."

I walked calmly down the dock, enjoying the breeze and lingering to admire the purple starfish clinging to the rocks in the clear water. John met me at the companionway entrance.

"You missed him!" he said excitedly.

"Where? Where?" I cried.

"He's gone," John said. "Gone until next Tuesday. Let that be a lesson to you. Relax your vigilance for a moment during the busy season, and he's gone. Nothing moves faster than a marine mechanic in the summer."

"'What the heck is this? Who installed this piece of junk?'" I said sadly. "Maybe someday I'll get to see him."

Happy Birthday

I AWAKENED HAPPY. WE were in a cosy slip at Secret Cove, 24 hours after a very expensive coupling repair, and it was my 47th birthday. I rolled over in the aft cabin and hugged my husband, who was lying beside me. "Wake up, darling. Do you know what day this is?"

John opened his eyes. For a moment he looked confused, then cautious. He kissed me affectionately. "My, I'm a lucky man, to have such a lovely wife," he said. "Have you lost a pound or two? You seem thinner."

"You're stalling, darling," I said. "You've forgotten."

"Forgotten? Forgotten? Would I forget ... my own wife's birthday?" He looked relieved and pleased with himself. He had the air of a man who had had a lucky escape.

"So what did you get me?" I asked.

Suddenly John looked uncomfortable. "I thought I'd take you for a boat ride," he said at last. He beamed at me happily.

I sagged limply into the mattress. Back across Georgia Strait? Back through the torpedo zone? "Maybe we'll bump into the dinghy we lost coming across," I said. When my sarcasm got no response, I added, "Lucky I put all my summer dresses in storage in Cowichan Bay. If the boat sinks I'll have something to live for."

John ignored me. "It'll be a birthday to remember," he said.

"Every birthday with you is memorable, darling," I said tactfully.

"Happy birthday," said John. "Get up. We have to get the boat ready."

"We really should use up some of our provisions before we head back, darling," I said.

"Oh all right," said John. "Fix me a hearty breakfast."

I raced to the port locker in the main saloon and pulled out a cookbook I hadn't yet tried — a gift from our friend Ed the Bald. Ed the Bald lived in a Tollycraft just down our dock at Cowichan Bay. Though new to boating, he had known John years before I did in the Arctic, and his sense of humour and pack-rat propensities were already part of the local folklore. So lovely of Ed to be helpful to a bride whose years of hopelessness in the galley were also fodder for Cowichan Bay gossip. As he'd handed me the cookbook, he'd explained that this was the latest edition, and told me that the deep-fried eggs were his personal favourite. I opened the binder reverently. *The Canadian Army Recipe Book — 1957.* I really should use up some of my flour and eggs. There — griddle cakes. I jotted the recipe on a scrap of paper.

> Yield: Approx 36 pounds batter
> 200 six-inch griddle cakes
> flour, pastry, sifted — 12 lb
> baking powder — 12 oz
> salt — 2 ½ tbsp
> eggs — 16 (approx 3 cups)
> sugar — 3 lb
> milk — 5 ½ qt
> vanilla — 4 tsp
> fat, melted — 2 lb

"Sixteen eggs," I thought. "I don't quite have enough ..." Then I looked at the yield. How silly of me! Why, 200 griddle cakes was 196 too many. I'd just have to divide the recipe by 50. Good thing I was always clever at math. Now, 12 pounds of flour divided by 50 ...

A short while later I had run out of paper. Maybe scrambled eggs would be better. I knew the upscale marina restaurant was serving mango chutney and crepes and eggs Benedict, and I wanted to compete with something more elegant than oatmeal mush. The words leaped out at me from the pages of the recipe book. A hundred and twenty-five eggs? I thought not. The math was too much for me. John interrupted my reverie.

"We've been here for 14 days, and it's boring. I'm glad we're going home."

"Boring?" I said, rummaging through a food locker. "Boring? How can you say such a thing? We've read six books each and eaten so many cashews our pants don't fit. Just yesterday we listened to that fascinating radio program about Finnish washerwomen who make music with squeaking dishcloths, and didn't you say yourself that giant muffin I made in the pressure cooker was absolutely delicious?"

"And last night for fun we swatted mosquitoes with charts," John said. "And I'm sick of canned ham and powdered beef stroganoff."

"I even wrote a poem," I said.

"When I cut my husband's hair he looks like Bert
And he complains throughout the coffee shop.
He says if he had feelings they'd be hurt.
He says it looks like Ernie cut his mop ..."

"Brilliant, my little dumpling," John said soothingly, "but I'm still glad to be going home. What's for breakfast?"

"Oatmeal mush," I said. "I had a wonderful time here. I found out you were once brother-in-law to Muktuk Annie, the Inuit heavy equipment operator famous for her partying, and I knit three pairs of socks. But you may be right. It may be time to return home. We're down to our last three potatoes and our last can of beans."

"One can of beans!" John exclaimed. "We might not make it. Can we get more before we leave?"

I ploughed on. "We made six new friends and ate spaghetti on the deck with them before they sailed away."

"Everyone sailed away except us," said John, "and now it's our turn."

We ate our breakfast and readied the boat. The sky was clear, the wind was brisk and the engine oil was topped up. Our Secret Cove neighbours came out of their boats to wish us farewell and cast off lines. I threw my arms around one neighbouring woman.

"Happy birthday," she said warmly.

"I don't feel 47," I said. "I feel terrified. But thanks."

The engine, safely in neutral, roared loudly. I busily coiled lines and the *Inuksuk* drifted away from the dock. John slipped the boat into forward gear and the bow, heavy and dependable, slid through the dark water. I strained my eyes to look behind me as Secret Cove slipped past us. The sun was hot. I took a deep breath as we ploughed through the water toward Georgia Strait. There was only four feet of chop, but the wind was on our nose and we'd have to motor.

I took the wheel, while the GPS danced us over the chart, and aimed the solidness of the *Inuksuk* toward Nanaimo Harbour. Did I feel courageous? Intrepid? Competent? No to all three, but I wasn't completely panicked either, and I was mildly optimistic we'd survive the trip.

I unzipped my cruiser suit partway down the front — I was starting to perspire. The rollers behind us rocked the boat from side to side. The seas appeared to be outrunning us, and the rocking unsettled me. Suddenly I wanted quiet. "I think I'll go below and rest, darling," I said. A wave washed over the deck. The seas were rising and the rocking motion increased.

I braced myself below amid falling books. *The Canadian Army Recipe Book — 1957* slid out of the bookshelf and landed on my head. I moaned a little, opened one eye and brushed the cookbook peevishly to the floor. Summoning the strength of my ancestors, I staggered to the head and looked at my face in the mirror. My tan stood out sharply on my face like a badly chosen shade of makeup. My eyes were sunken, my hair was wild and a fine sheen of perspiration stood out on my skin. My eyes seemed to have trouble focussing. There was something wrong with my digestion, but I didn't want to think about it. Maybe if I put it from my mind ... Lurching through the clutter on the floor of the violently moving main saloon, I climbed the companionway and presented my pale face to my husband.

John, radiant with happiness, was standing firmly behind the wheel. His glasses were bespeckled with salt spray, and he was well into the third verse of a sea chanty. "John," I croaked.

He broke off singing and looked at me. "Are you fixing lunch?" he asked cheerfully. "I feel a bit peckish."

I didn't reply. I crawled into the cockpit, snapped on my safety harness and retched wretchedly over the side of the boat. "Are you all right?" John asked.

"Never better," I replied, as another wave of nausea overtook me. "Continue singing, if you like, but quietly. Have some respect for the dying."

"Are you seasick?" John asked helplessly, torn between the wheel and his distressed crew.

"You'll find my affairs in order, I think," I said. "Divide my jewellery among our daughters, organize a tasteful cremation and scatter my ashes over Cowichan Bay. If you can get my body that far. They'll say I was young — only 47 and in my prime. My biggest regret is that I'll die before I get to be thin." Another spasm overtook me. "If this trip had lasted another month, I would have pared down another two dress sizes at least. Wish me a happy birthday, my love, and kiss me before I pass out. Whose idea was this trip anyway?"

"I'm not kissing the first mate who's just been sick over the side of the boat," John said firmly. "Even if it is her birthday."

When we approached Nanaimo, the water and my stomach had settled a little. The crackling radio told of boats rafted up alongside each other at the marina. We were weary and salt-sprayed and our red-rimmed eyes searched out space in the quiet nesting of boats at Newcastle Marine Park. I positioned myself on the bow, loosened the mud-encrusted anchor and waited for John's signal. It took four tries. The third time I winched the anchor chain up, I was convinced I was even closer to glory than when I was seasick. When the fourth drop took, I staggered weakly down the companionway, crawled on my hands and knees for the starboard settee berth and lay full length on the cushions, shaking and exhausted and gasping.

John leaned over and kissed me warmly. "Happy birthday, my little dumpling," he said. "What's for supper?"

"Oatmeal mush," I said feebly. "Unless, of course, the captain wants to cook dinner himself."

We feasted on our last three potatoes and a can of beans. Happy birthday. We were safe at anchor. It really was a happy birthday.

Panic Attack

"Such a shame, John," I said.

"What's a shame?" John asked.

"That we have no talent for nude sunbathing and sipping gin." We were sitting in the cockpit of the *Inuksuk* at Clam Bay, anchored gently on the muddy bottom. The encircling arms of Thetis Island made a lovely haven halfway between Nanaimo and Cowichan Bay. I sighed softly and slipped out of my size large popsicle-orange cruiser suit, exposing a rumpled T-shirt and stained jeans. My ears were sunburned and my face felt scratchy.

We'd shot through Dodds Narrows exactly on slack tide. I was proud that I'd developed a new technique for tackling the narrows. It was the "close-your-eyes-and-concentrate-on-saying-nothing" technique, and it had worked like a charm. A whiff of diesel, the sun beating on my Secret Cove souvenir hat, sheer rocks sloping dangerously down (I peeked a little), brisk breeze, boats flying out all over, and we were through. John was perfectly capable of handling the *Inuksuk* by himself, and my job was to not make an almighty nuisance of myself. John had kindly explained all this to me over a romantic, candle-lit dinner of corned beef, rice and grape juice the night before. I had sunk into his arms with gratitude, weak with relief. My constant vigilance, nervous twitchings and cries of alarm were superfluous to the smooth operation of the boat! Panic was optional. The sense of relief nearly settled my stomach.

We had a straight run down Thetis Passage toward Thetis Island with our exhaust gently outrunning us, and I stood courageously at the helm, hardly a ripple on the water and the sun blazing on the great glassy surface, glistening for miles. I had confidently burst into an a capella chorus of "Yo ho ho and a bottle of rum" when suddenly our GPS skewed back toward Dodds Narrows, like Lot's wife. John hurriedly began to reprogram the machine, but it seemed determined to point us back in the direction from which we had come. He gave up on the GPS and was just plotting a compass course toward Clam Bay, ready to con his way into the anchorage, when the crew turned into a pillar of salt.

"I can't stand it!" I yelled. "Every time we go out, something goes wrong. My last nerve has snapped. I'm jumping ship. Let me off at the next port. I'll move into a cardboard box if I have to. I was calm when the anchor chain slipped. I didn't complain the first time the coupling broke. I hardly murmured when we ventured into a torpedo firing range and lost the dinghy, and the engine leak barely disturbed me. I was a good sport the second time the coupling broke, and when I had to anchor four times in Newcastle Marine Park, I didn't utter a word of reproach but this is too much!" My voice crescendoed and the crew of a passing sailboat gave me a nervous look. "If we hadn't lost the dinghy, I'd crawl into it and row into the sunset," I yelled. "Well, haven't you got anything to say?"

"A wise man says nothing," said John. "Isn't that Clam Bay?"

"Clam Bay?" I sobbed. "Clam Bay? Are we there?"

"We are there," John said firmly. "If you've finished, I'll need help anchoring. When I signal, drop the anchor to the bottom, wave to me to back up, set out more chain, tighten the winch and chop with your hands to let me know to stop the boat when the anchor catches."

I stared at John, shocked into a cessation of sobbing. "You mean there's a *way* to *do* it?" I said. "I thought I just dropped the anchor, and we yelled at each other a few times, fended off the boats we nearly hit, pulled up the anchor and tried again somewhere new."

"Well, there *is* a bit of a technique to it," John admitted.

"And the reason you've never shared any of this with me is ... ?" My voice was dangerously snotty.

"I thought you knew how to do it," John said weakly.

"Darling," I explained, "it should be fairly obvious after my four attempts at anchoring last night that I'm an idiot at this."

We spotted the markers and gently nosed our way into the anchorage. The diesel engine throbbed.

With great dignity I picked my way forward and hunched over the anchor. We prowled among the pretty anchored boats as stealthily as a cougar, while John sniffed out the perfect position. Our strained and intent faces created a sensation on several of the anchored boats, and the crews eyed us edgily. Suddenly we spotted an obvious bare patch well in front of a little white ketch. John raised his arm and ... the anchoring went without a hitch.

I strolled to the cockpit exuding confidence.

"Yes," I said later. "Gin and nude sunbathing. I'm ready for the next frontier. I think I'm getting a handle on this sailboat thing. In fact, I'm getting quite good at it."

Home Again

"I miss the TV," said John. "You made me leave it behind."

"It's good for you," I said. "Too much TV rots your brain. I miss going for coffee at the Starfish Studio."

"Well, we'll be home tomorrow," John said. "A straight run down Sansum Narrows and we're there."

We were anchored in Clam Bay on Thetis Island. We were enjoying the calm water and the warmth of the last sunrays of the day. We'd finished a delicious dinner of rice and canned ham and apples.

"When we get home, I'm going straight to bed and I'm going to stay there for three days. Post-traumatic stress disorder is a terrible thing and I can feel a case of it coming on. I want to get e-mail," I continued, "and mail. I want to visit thrift stores and discuss you with all my girlfriends. I want to get where I'm going by car. Cars don't need to be anchored. You don't have to wash the salt off them every night. You don't have to drag a dinghy behind them. You don't have to drive through torpedo zones. You don't have to —"

"I get the picture," John said. "Didn't you have a good time?"

"Of course, my love," I said. "I'm having a good time now, for example, since I'm not retching violently over the side of the cockpit."

"I knew you had a good time," John said confidently.

"I wonder if Screaming Liver bought that old wooden boat," I said.

"It's rotten as a pear," said John.

"Everyone at Cowichan Bay says that about everyone's boat but their own," I said. "If you listened to the scuttlebutt, you'd be astonished the whole marina isn't sunk."

"I *am* astonished the whole marina isn't sunk," John said, peering around the hard dodger. "That little ketch behind us is acting funny. She seems to have a lot of anchor rode out, and I think her tackle may be light."

"I don't mean to influence your decision or anything," I said, "but resetting the anchor would most likely kill me."

"It's probably all right," John said. "Let's get some sleep. We're out of here early."

I took one last look at the lingering twilight. Clam Bay was all tree edges and multicoloured highlights. The sky was clear and the darkling crept nearer, muddying the surface as the water swayed gently in the quiet. One crow called to another and a heron, stiff-legged even in flight, let loose a raucous cry as it flapped awkwardly past. Our holiday was nearly done. I had only to live through tomorrow, and we would have made it safely home. I sighed, then went below.

The next morning, I hastily boiled a handful or two of oatmeal on our propane stovetop, making a mental note to forever strike oatmeal from my diet after this trip was over. And canned ham. And bread and margarine. And bananas. John called excitedly down the companionway. "Catherine! Come look at this!" I twitched violently and slopped oatmeal on myself.

"Tell me we're not sinking," I yelled, and I ran up the ladder.

"We're not sinking at all," John said. "Look at the GPS! It's working perfectly! And after yesterday too, when it went all funny!"

"And the first mate burst into hysterics and mutinied on the spot — it's coming back to me now," I said.

"I was too polite to mention that part," John said. "My, but you're excitable."

"Let's go home, darling," I said. The words fell from my lips like a prayer. "Let's go home."

The little white ketch behind us had held her position all night, and our anchor slid up so easily it was an omen. "Born to winch," I commented to John once I was back in the cockpit. The afternoon we'd spent at the Nanaimo dock laying out yards of anchor chain, yelling at each other, untangling knots of steel and reversing the chain had paid off. The breeze ruffled our hair and stung our eyes a little. The motor throbbed strongly as we made our way steadily south. The bow cut neatly through the water, the sun shone enthusiastically and I became more and more confident as familiar landmarks slid past. "The cables," I said. "Maple Bay." And almost reverently, "Cherry Point." Suddenly we were approaching Cowichan Bay. "Starboard or port dock?" I asked John.

"First let's see if someone's in our slip," John said. "This is Cowichan Bay. You never know."

The slip was clear. Tears misted my eyes. There were so many volunteers to help us dock, I was hard pressed to throw enough lines to give everyone something to do. Arms reached out to cradle the *Inuksuk* back to her home. Jean-Paul secured the stern line, as if to give brackets to our trip — he had been the one to release it when we left.

Ed the Bald helped me step onto the dock. "So what went wrong?" he asked, with a grin. "Anything? According to the rumours I heard, you're lucky to be alive, let alone floating."

"It's a long story," said John. "Buy us a coffee and we'll tell you all about it." We were home. Intact. Broke. Still married.

Delilah of the Docks

It WAS A calm, sunny morning. I stretched myself slowly, then reached for my coffee mug. "We're home, darling." I said. "Back in Cowichan Bay."

"I need a haircut," said John. "Will you cut my hair for me?"

I popped the last piece of toast into my mouth. "Oh, all right. Where are the scissors?" I dug in the head locker and came out waving them.

"Careful with those," said John. "Last time you cut my hair, you slashed one of my ears."

"The merest nick," I said. "Wrap this towel around your neck."

"To absorb the blood?" John asked.

I sniffed and made my first cut, dramatically, across his bangs. Soon a billowing cascade of iron-grey hair floated and danced over the teak-and-holly floor. John was crouched on a little stool, head down, eyes squeezed shut and both hands clamped over his ears.

"You can look now, darling," I said. "I'm done." John released his ears and looked about him.

"You know," he said, "I may be turning a little grey."

"Darling," I said, "you've been grey for the five years I've known and loved you."

"I'm brown and blond on top," John said.

"And I'm a natural redhead," I said soothingly. "Go look at yourself in the mirror. And when you do, remember that the price was right."

I snapped the scissors shut. John cringed and reached instinctively for his ears.

As I swept up the fallen locks, I could hear an exclamation from the head. "I did a good job, didn't I, darling?" I called.

"I look like a convict," John said. I swept another broomful of hair fluff into the dustpan. "If I was a teenager, I'd run away from home."

"We spent all our money in Secret Cove," I said. "Expect homemade haircuts for the next while. Couplings don't come cheap." John emerged from the head with a dismal expression on his face. "There's a little tuft under that ear — let me clip it — and that bald spot will grow back. Too late to do anything about your sideburns."

"Where's my hat?" John asked.

"You going out, my love?" I asked.

"No," he said. "Can't go out. Can't be seen in public for at least a month."

"You've suffered no major disfigurement," I said.

"I have too," John said.

"All I need is a little practice, darling. Besides, you're better off than Ed the Bald, who has no hair at all. And German Bob has to *pay* someone to cut his hair. No one has ever seen Iron Mike without a baseball cap on, so it's one of the mysteries of Cowichan Bay as to whether he has any hair or not. Stafford the Respectable is the only resident of Cowichan Bay with nice hair. Naval John has to cut his own hair. He was a barber in the navy."

"He was? Maybe he'd cut my hair."

"He who defects from his wife to another haircutter gets no more free haircuts. It's a rule I learned from my neighbour. Fred once went to a hairdresser to 'fix' one of her haircuts, and she nearly stabbed him with the scissors. By accident, of course. Then there's Jean-Paul, the South Pacific veteran. He doesn't cut his hair at all."

"I wonder how I'd look in a ponytail."

"Divorced, because I wouldn't be seen dead in a ditch with you in a ponytail."

"But you'd be seen with me in a haircut like this?"

"It's hard to explain, darling, but it's kind of a mark of ownership — like a hand-knit sweater, or that we have matching raincoats when we go out together."

"I'm flattered."

"Besides, this is the haircut that makes you look like a resident of Cowichan Bay. A tourist would recognize you as a local immediately. We are home, darling, where this brand of creativity is greeted with the same sort of kindly laughter that greeted us when we clipped Fred's boat, when we painted our deck diaper brown, and when we melted our engine and had to be towed home. Darling, this is where we live, and this is the haircut that gives you that unmistakable Cowichan Bay stamp. A man of the sea — a man who laughs at convention — a man brave enough and defiant enough to let his wife cut his hair."

"Can I cut your hair, then?"

"Don't be silly, darling."

Ed the Bald poked his head down our companionway. "A haircut!" he exclaimed. "John's got a haircut! Hey Fred, Mike — come look at this!"

"We're home, my love," I said. "We're back in the bay."

Back in the Bay

"FOLKS, THIS IS Cowichan Bay, and I am your tour guide and wildlife officer. Now watch your step down this ramp. Safe?" (light laugh) "Well, it's never actually collapsed — at least, not recently. Hang on to your purses and keys. I once dropped my knitting bag into the sea off this ramp. A sock and a half, and my favourite needles! I'd have thrown myself in after them, but my husband stopped me.

"To your left, or should I say 'port,' is a tiny, exquisite, two-storey floathome. At low tide it rests on the mud and leans sideways. The last woman who lived there positively stormed out of the floathome and into a townhouse, which had been built with a carpenter's level. We all felt she was a little unreasonable. After all, the head works. You just have to cling to the toilet paper dispenser or you fall into the shower. This floathome is for sale. It's slightly larger than a walk-in closet. We have no idea why the owners would want to part with such a treasure. We call this colour 'blush.' The waterline?" (close inspection) "Oh — we call that 'scum.'

"Now here's the floathome *Duck Sloop*, haunt of Stafford the Respectable. Some of us just walk to the beat of a different drummer. Stafford stands apart." (lowered voice) "He has a *job*." (pause for effect) "*And* he takes regular baths. Note the tidy front porch and the outdoor seawater aquarium. Most of us aren't organized enough to keep fish longer than it takes to eat them, but Stafford has a fascination for living fish. He kayaks, you know. When we have our Christmas sailpast, Stafford paddles past with six electric lights and a battery pack. But he's all right.

"Now directly across from Stafford the Respectable is Blaine the Merchant. Need an extra-long stainless-steel bolt for a stanchion repair? Blaine has three to choose from. Then he'll sell you a second-hand drill, a rusty toolbox to store it in and a hand vacuum cleaner to suck up the cement dust afterward. If you mention in passing that your grandchildren are visiting that afternoon, well, he happens to have some children's life jackets on special. Then he'll sell you some pie (kids like dessert) and he has an old wheelbarrow — for you a special price — to cart all the stuff down the dock to your boat. Make way — make way — here's another dazed-looking customer with a wheelbarrow full of loot. Blaine rolls his own cigarettes and shaves every second day, but you've never met such a terrific salesman. If he ever turned his talents to Mary Kay Cosmetics, there'd be a pink Cadillac parked in Cowichan Bay and all the locals would be wearing the right shade of lipstick.

"Right next to Blaine the Merchant are the two Muffin Ladies. The Muffin Ladies have been known to bake apple pies for Screaming Liver. They're two older ladies who think Screaming Liver is a very nice young man who should balance out all that beer with vitamin C. They bought their boat from Naval John, who moved into an apartment with a bathtub and rugs. Unlike the rest of us, they actually go places in their little boat, and they keep it painted and ship-shape. It was the Muffin Ladies who hosted the First Annual Cowichan Bay Muffin Festival. This is the civilized end of the dock.

"Here is Ed the Bald and his Tollycraft. Ed knew my husband when John had money. And then John had an art gallery. And then he didn't have money or the art gallery. Ed the Bald, who owns as much stuff as Blaine the Merchant, wants it on record that even though he was with my husband in Value Village 15 years ago when John picked out his orange shorts, he takes no responsibility for them. In fact, he says he tried to talk him out of them. I am suspicious of this claim, but I still like Ed the Bald.

"Next to Ed the Bald is Cowichan Bay's own Oktoberfest. Starts every November and runs for 12 months. Screaming Liver is your host. On this finger are three boats, belonging to Ed the Bald, Iron Mike and Screaming Liver. Don't step on Iron Mike's potted plants or on Joey the Sheltie Dog. The festivities begin every day at the crack of noon and end when the last dog is hung. Nothing personal, Joey.

"Moving right along, we get to the *Wun Wey*. Jean-Paul stands apart as the only resident of Cowichan Bay who has sailed south far enough to melt his butter. He's lived through storms so horrible even the sharks were frightened, and eaten papayas fresh off the tree in secluded lagoons with the sun as loving as a mother, and the swell rocking the boat as gently as a grandmother putting a child to bed. Endis, his wife, was too shy to get off the boat for the first year, but we love her to pieces. In her village on the island of Efete in Vanuatu you are not supposed to enter a dwelling unless you are invited. She was too timid to invite us onboard her boat, and we couldn't catch more than a glimpse of her because she'd slip down the companionway before we could shout 'Hello!' Angelique, their daughter, is by contrast an extrovert. She stands on the deck on her sturdy, three-year-old legs and hollers 'Hi!' and 'Bye!' to everyone who passes. They are the only two words of English she knows. She also yells in French and pidgin, but we don't understand French and pidgin as well as English. We listen to Jean-Paul's stories, then drift off to join Oktoberfest. Bye! Bye! Bye! Angelique, you can stop now. Bye! Bye! Bye honey! Bye!

"Across the way is Older-Than-Dirt Don's trimaran. Older-Than-Dirt has coffee every morning with German Bob. The two men were on opposite sides of WW II, and whenever German Bob says anything to annoy Older-Than-Dirt Don, he raises his arm, aims it like a rifle and says, 'Bob, if you were six inches taller, 50 years ago I'd have nailed you right between the eyes.' Then they both laugh crazily and ask the waitress for more coffee.

"Our neighbour and her husband, Fred, live aboard the *Abdi*. The geraniums belong to our neighbour and the fibreglass patches belong to Fred. Our neighbour says that a fibreglass-over-wood deck takes constant maintenance — just like Fred — and that if she ever died Fred would be married to a waitress within three months because he can't cook. She says that a really cunning man would marry the cook, but Fred doesn't think that far ahead, and he'd never make it past the waitress. Note the cat litter box nestled among the geranium pots. We feel this adds character.

"Here is Murray's boat — proudly ferrocement just like ours. The stanchions are pink. His wife, Judy, felt she needed to make a statement — like my crocheted skull-and-crossbones porthole covers, or our neighbour's ironed curtains or Marilyn's home-baked bread or Shirley's petunias in an old head and a pair of Craig's discarded boots.

"This is our boat, the *Inuksuk*. You'll notice that our deck is a tasteful blend of blues, greys and creams. The hull is navy blue, the boot top is white ... you can't see the boot top on the port side? No, it's not the angle you're looking from, it's the list of the boat. Those white splashes on the deck? We don't talk about them. That slime in the water? We don't talk about that either.

"Let me direct you attention to the *Shogun*. Geoff and Marilyn and Nika the pit bull live aboard her. *Shogun* was once a WW II air crew recovery vessel. Big, isn't she? She's almost the age of Older-Than-Dirt Don, and she's just as feisty. Twin diesels and great masses of power, sort of like a Zamboni with class. Marilyn is an excellent cook. We like her a lot.

"At the end of the dock is German Bob's sloop. The *Vondoit* bounces a lot because she's on the outermost slip. We think German Bob likes the excitement. On stormy days it makes us seasick just to watch his bow dive under the water and then shoot skyward.

"And that's our dock. On your way back, be careful not to trip on any wires. It's a little messy underfoot, what with the telephone wires and electrical wires and water lines and cable lines and such-like.

This dock is not up to the aesthetic standard of really classy docks, like Nanaimo or Sidney, but we like it here, and most of us like each other. Bad weather brings everyone out to stand on the docks and look worried, and most summer days you'll find us repairing our boats. Evenings, we gather to discuss our husbands and which heads have broken down. Weekends, we hide from tourists. I had hoped more of our neighbours would come out, but even John was below today. He's not in a very good mood. He thinks public tours and books and admitting eccentricities are a really bad idea, and probably most of our neighbours are away consulting lawyers."

German Bob

THE SUN WAS unexpectedly hot for August. We had fled from the bowels of the *Inuksuk* to catch the wispy breeze coming off the water. A rumpled-looking figure walked briskly down the dock toward us with his baseball cap shading his head. His eyes were focussed in front of him with fierce contemplation, and on his face there was a scowl.

"Here comes German Bob," said John. "Repeat after me — quick! *Guten tag mein klein Deutsche blumen.*"

"*Guten tag mein klein Deutsche blumen,*" I said obediently. "What does it mean?"

"Good day, my little German flower. Say it to German Bob."

"No!" I gasped. "He'll throw me in the sea!"

"Go ahead," said John.

"He'll never speak to me again!"

"Live recklessly," said John.

"Oh, all right." I said. I turned to Bob who had just nodded brusquely at us on his way past. "*Guten tag mein klein Deutsche blumen.*"

German Bob stopped as suddenly as if he'd been shot. He turned an astonished face toward me, swallowed twice and attempted to smile. The failure was spectacular. His natural aversion to other people's wives wrestled with his lonesome mariner's chivalry. A fleeting impulse to clout me over the head visibly crossed his face, then he swung his head to look for an escape route. "John put me up to it, Bob," I said placatingly.

"Uh huh," he said weakly, and hustled off to his boat as quickly as he could.

I turned to my husband. "German Bob is swift-tongued in two languages. That's the first time I've ever seen him at a loss for words. And it really was unkind of me to tease him — the only female he ever loved was his old dog Cindy." I paused. "Cindy was nicer than me," I added thoughtfully.

"Better looking, too," said my husband. "Wetter nose."

"Gentler, kinder, less judgmental and friendlier," I continued. "Loyal, sweet-natured and eloquent in her silent regard for all mankind, though she was perhaps more pointed in her attentions to those of us who had dog biscuits. Yes, Cindy was humble, obedient and loving. That dog was a Christian. German Bob never got over her passing. The only dog I've ever met who is as sweet as Cindy was is old Joey, the mangy sheltie who belongs to Ed the Bald. Such a shame Ed doesn't have time to walk him."

John and I simultaneously turned our heads to look at each other. "German Bob used to take Cindy for long walks." John said. "He took excellent care of her. Remember how he used to slip us biscuits to feed Cindy?"

"Is devotion to a dog transferable?" I asked. "I mean, German Bob's a little rough around the edges, but he's kind to children and animals, and I bet he'd love to walk Joey. It's people he can't stand."

And so the tide turned at Cowichan Bay. German Bob walked Joey nearly every day — long walks and swims down by the beach and rambles up the hill. The old dog was grateful and lumbered to his feet every time the old mariner and his pocketful of biscuits arrived at his dock.

Yesterday German Bob and Joey met me coming down the ramp. "*Guten tag*, Bob," I said genially. "Hi, Joey."

German Bob reached into his pocket and handed me a biscuit.

"Here," he said. "Give it to Joey." His bewhiskered face shone with a simple happiness.

Joey looked up at him adoringly. I gave Joey his treat, then made my way down the dock. There may not be much that's flower-like about a cranky old salt like German Bob, but he's okay.

Chores at the Bay

It was Saturday morning in Cowichan Bay. The wind was brisk and the sky was clear, but not one sail could we see out on the bay. "I think I'll take a stroll down the dock to see who's doing what," I said to John. "Come with me, darling?"

"I could be talked into a walk," said John.

We climbed off the *Inuksuk*, briefly balancing atop the wooden block on the dock just abeam of the boat. Last winter I had come to grief on that identical block, landing face down on the dock with one shoe off and my briefcase clutched heroically in one fist. I didn't get any sympathy from the neighbours. "Dock okay?" our neighbour Fred had asked. Winter had been grey and chilly and wet and slick, and summer had been hot, but now it was an unexpectedly warm day in fall and all the people in Cowichan Bay were sunning themselves — along with lines full of flapping laundry.

We strolled arm in arm down the dock, past power lines, crumbly concrete and creaking boards, and Nika the pit bull at the end of the dock barking out of sheer boredom. We spotted German Bob on the deck of his boat.

I grabbed John's arm. "He's *painting* his *deck!*" I said in an excited whisper. "German Bob's boat hasn't been painted since Older-Than-Dirt Don did the hull for him three years ago!" We stopped to gape, too astonished to be polite. The boat's hull was dull gunmetal grey, but the deck was shiny and yellow in the morning sunshine. German

Bob slopped his roller around a winch and shuffled farther back, squatting low to the deck.

"Thought it was about time," he said happily. "And it's a good day for it." We tore ourselves away from his boat, stunned into silence.

Jean-Paul was silently stripping the interior of his boat and we poked our heads inside to say hello. Piles of teak lay strewn about the dock, along with rusty tanks. Jean-Paul looked at them proudly. "A little welding and you're done," John said. Jean-Paul grunted in reply, and bent back to his work.

Farther down the dock, we saw our neighbour on the deck of her boat, stringing floor mats across the boom. "Ahoy, neighbour," I called. "How are you?"

"Ahoy yourself," she said. "Buddy the cat has disgraced himself again. It's Fred's fault. He likes the cat, so it's his fault. I'm giving the floor rugs their daily wash. I hate cats. I don't like rugs. In fact, I'm not fond of husbands either." She clambered barefoot off her boat and joined us on the dock, her laughing face brown and her hair bright in the sun. "I went to the doctor the other day," she said.

"The doctor!" I gasped. "Are you all right?"

"Just a checkup," she said. "I told the doctor sometimes I feel the urge to hold Fred's head under water until he stops thrashing, but I didn't think it was serious because the feeling usually passes. I asked the doctor if she thought it was menopause. She didn't even laugh. She asked if I'd ever considered marriage counselling. Me! Marriage counselling! I've been married so long I'm an expert at it."

"Where's Fred now?" John asked.

"He left about the same time I started cleaning rugs. I think he's hiding in the shop."

"We'll head down the dock to see him," John said. "I want to see how your engine is coming along."

We strolled a few slips farther and paused to watch Ed the Bald slap fibreglass on the starboard side of his boat.

"Patching that hole?" John called.

"Well, if it isn't the Dooks of Hazard," Ed drawled. "It's a hole no more. The minute this baby dries, and I hope it's before Christmas …" He squinted at the sky. "Rain, d'ya think?" Ed the Bald shares a dock with Iron Mike, who was out tending his tomatoes. Iron Mike has the healthiest-looking tomato plants I've ever seen. He looks as fierce as an axe-murderer, and when he started his box garden on the dock nobody believed he wasn't growing exotic herbs illegal in this country. But not only was he just growing tomatoes, his face glows when he talks about them.

"Rain'll hold off, Ed," he said softly, then turned back to his gardening.

"Good-looking plants," I said.

"Cherry tomatoes," Mike said, and nearly smiled. "These are good, but I'm looking to get some European tomato seeds next year."

Steve, also known as Screaming Liver, popped his head up from the cockpit of his tiny wooden cutter. "Hi Mom. Hi Dad," he said.

"Steve," I said, "I hate to break this to you, but we're all the same age. We're not your parents."

"I can always hope," he said. "I heard you could cook, Mom."

"That's just a rumour," said John.

"Now cut that out, Dad. Stop teasing Mom like that. Care to join me in a beer?"

"Thanks, Steve, but I never drink before noon," I said.

"What a coincidence. Neither do I," he said. "It's two minutes after twelve."

We walked up the creaking ramp toward Fred's shop. Fred was painting parts for the engine he planned to put in his boat. He looked at the engine block proudly. It was cleaner than my galley, and the surface shimmered gently in the glow of the overhead light bulbs. "Wife's on a rampage," he said easily. "Isn't she a beauty?"

"The wife or the engine block?" I asked.

"Both," he said hastily. "Just look at this, John." He held out a newly painted green injector pump.

I drifted back toward the *Inuksuk*. Beautiful sailing weather, and nobody in Cowichan Bay was sailing.

Then from the cluster of masts at the marina, I saw a movement. A mast tip glided purposefully out into the bay. Below it was a patched sail and a small wooden cutter with one side painted and the other bare. (Iron Mike, doing the chore for Steve, had never got around to painting the other side.) On the deck stood Steve, engineless, crewless and manoeuvring his boat through the marina under sail. He waved his arm and shouted. I caught a glimpse of his grin, then he was gone to play boats — to sail doughnuts out in the bay, and catch the evening turn of the wind back into his slip.

John and I returned to the *Inuksuk* to tidy the boat and scrub the deck. I looked over my shoulder at him. I was on my hands and knees polishing a dorade.

"Darling," I said to him, "of all the wise people at Cowichan Bay, which of us is the wisest? The clever folk who fix their boats, or the sailor-lad who goes to sea when the wind is right and the sun shines on his brightwork — even if it's peeling? I wonder, sometimes."

Hobbies for Liveaboards

WHEN I LIVED on land, my life was filled with hobbies that took up space. Like stamp collecting. And since I've moved onto a boat, I feel mildly guilty that I'm not out there every day in my little dinghy tending crab pots, learning how to fish for ling cod, finding out what a ling cod looks like in its wild state, rinsing the mooring lines in fresh water, skinny-dipping off the stern of the boat by moonlight, diving with the snorkelling gear my husband gave me last Christmas to check the zincs, climbing the mast to fix the loud hailer … These are the activities of an exuberant woman half my age and width. Being of ponderous middle age, I reserve my enthusiasm for activities within the range of my abilities.

One of my favourite pastimes, introduced to me by my neighbour, is the art of interpreting the bird droppings on our deck. Some women read tea leaves. We women of the docks have grown far beyond such childish games. As soon as the starling droppings turn a startling shade of purple, the blackberries down by the lawn tennis club are ripe. I share this information not to boast of my abilities, but to allow women within range of blackberries everywhere to expand their repertoire of wisdom.

Another gift we women of the docks possess is that of communicating with the aforesaid starlings. The starlings sit in our rigging and laugh and laugh and defecate all over our decks while we women of Cowichan Bay dance at the foot of our masts and threaten them — sort of like a group of hostile Dr. Doolittles. My neighbour slaps her mast and threatens to wake up her sleepy Siamese cat, Buddy, and I wave broom handles and yell, while the starlings loudly and obviously sneer at us. Then they call on all their friends to come and see what the excitement is about, and soon there is a Hallelujah Chorus of starlings sitting in the rigging saying things like, "This is really fun. Let's call Pete. Hey, Pete!" On land I'd never experienced this kind of communion with nature.

Another activity I enjoy is predicting the weather. It would be beneath me to step into the cockpit, look around and assess conditions. True to the traditions of the dock, we at Cowichan Bay do things the hard way. I tune in our little marine radio to raise the local weather station. "My heavens, John!" I gasp. "I can't raise Saltspring Island! The tower's been knocked down by a typhoon! We're going to die! The docks'll break up and the whole marina will end up three miles inland!"

"It's channel 2," John says.

"Oh," I say.

"And it's early fall," says John, "and the boat's not rocking."

"So should I wear my high heels or my sneakers?" I ask.

"Well, is it raining?" John asks.

"Let me check the station," I say.

What we at Cowichan Bay lack in common sense we compensate for in technical ability. Yes, when enormous waves with crests on top of them roll into the bay, there are people standing on the heaving docks in bewildered clusters. "This wasn't on the marine weather report. Oops! Charlie just fell in." We rely on our radios.

Something else at which the middle-aged boatwives of our dock excel is the art of washing and drying cushions and mats. My neighbour is particularly adept at this one and the rest of us are motivated by guilt when she sets the example. If her boat is festooned with drying carpets and flapping linen, we are galvanized into action. We pull out our buckets or descend on the local laundromat with armfuls of cushion covers, agonizing over decisions about vinegar and detergent brands, anxious to compete in camouflaging our booms with laundry. At Cowichan Bay this is a status symbol. The cleanest boatwives have laundry covered with bird droppings.

Something I've done more of than I ever did as a landlubber is the chore of ironing. My hanging lockers, full of condensation, drips and dropped plastic hangers, seem determined to compress my entire wardrobe into a kind of homogenized crumpled ball. Ironing onboard takes skill. First you have to have water. If the hoses on the dock are frozen or your husband was wildly extravagant during his last shower and your water tanks are empty, you may have to borrow a cup of water from your neighbour. Then you need to find a large dry towel to fold on the saloon table. If, during his shower, your husband has used all the towels too, you will have to borrow a towel from the same neighbour. Now a towel may seem like a rather personal article to borrow from a neighbour, but she has lockers too and she well understands your desperate need to iron.

Next, you dig your iron out from under your partly dried cushion covers — the ones you rescued from the starlings — and find an outlet to plug it in. Turn everything off, or you will be responsible for the next fried plug on the docks. Frying plugs is a skill we all possess, but we try to space out these exciting highlights — like birthdays, falling overboard and the kind of weather that breaks up the docks. You can get to the actual ironing after you've cleaned the stack of magazines, the candelabra, the CD player, your cell phone and four bills off the saloon table. The clever boatwife never irons more than one outfit at a time. There is a wrinkling force loose in her clothing lockers, and one iron, though a formidable weapon in the hands of a determined woman, can only do so much. Clothing ironed and then returned to a locker has mere minutes before it reverts to its pre-ironed state.

The Cowichan Bay woman has many activities with which to occupy herself. John rips a stamp off the phone bill. "Didn't you used to collect stamps?" he asks.

"Yes, my love," I answer, "but that was in another life. I think I'll go up on deck and look at bird droppings."

All of the Above

JOHN CAME OUT of the head sighing hugely. "It's not fair," he murmured. "It's not fair at all." He shook his head.

"What's not fair?" I asked.

"Other men have so little and I have so much," he said. "It's not fair. I am:

        a. handsome;

        b. charming;

        c. clever; or

        d. All of the above.

Sometimes 'all of the above' is the right answer."

"I know what you mean," I said. "Just last weekend I challenged the safe-boating certificate exam and got 34 right out of 36."

"I think you mentioned it," John said.

"The first three questions were easy," I said, "but the fourth was a tricky one about cardinal buoys. I searched my memory, and I recalled that the 'w' marker is spread out like a 'w' so logically the 'e' marker should be the exact opposite and the long surfaces would be against each other and the points at opposite ends — like two candy kisses end to end."

"I recall you telling me about that one too," said John. "At some length."

"So I guessed 'b.' I felt fairly confident about my decision, but all my senses were on alert. The first four had been in the 'a/b' range, so even though I didn't have a clue about the fifth question, I was sure the answer was 'c' or 'd.' I examined my options carefully. Should the captain check the weather and count life jackets prior to departure, or should he check the provisions?"

"I recall you telling me about this too," said John. "At some length."

"Well, I know provisions are important, especially for a long trip, but this was a safe-boating exam and any mention of life jackets immediately sends up a red flag — right? So I guessed 'c' and I was right on the money."

"Can we talk about something else?" John asked. There was a faint note of desperation in his voice.

"Of course, my darling," I said. "I did go on about it a little on the way home from the boat show last weekend."

"It was a three-hour trip," John said, "and I remember every word you said. Clearly."

"Do you remember me telling you about the fog question?" I asked.

"Oh yes," John said. "That was one of my favourites."

"Do you remember how I finessed the question about how to put a life jacket on in the water?"

"I think I had a dream about it last night," John said.

"Do you recall the part where the cell phone rang halfway through question 18 and I ordered a CD and guessed 'a' simultaneously? I remembered 'red right returning.' "

"How could I forget?" John asked. "My own snoggy-lipped wife is practically a genius. I wonder if the Starfish Studio is open yet? I think I'll go see." He hastily clambered up the companionway.

"And question 26!" I exclaimed. "A white light at night can mean almost anything — an anchored sailboat, a powerboat with the port and starboard lights burned out coming at you, a powerboat stern light pulling away from you — how was I to know? I agonized for what seemed like hours, and finally decided on 'd' — 'all of the above.' It was a fortunate guess. Every now and then 'all of the above' is the right answer."

"I'll keep that in mind," John said. "Can I go now?"

"Of course, my darling," I said. "But first let me tell you about question 31."

"I think not," John said. "Forget the test and come with me for coffee."

"What's wrong?" I asked.

"Choose one," John said. "I am:
     a. bored;
     b. satiated;
     c. fed up; or
     d. all of the above."

John leaned toward me and kissed me. "Sometimes 'all of the above' is the right answer."

Bilge-Rot and Social Status

"MY DARLING," I said, "I don't smell like most substitute teachers."

"Is this leading up to something?" John asked suspiciously.

"I don't mean to complain, but I think we have a case of bilge-rot and it's starting to affect my earning potential. A perfume wafts in front of me and lingers after I leave. Some teachers smell like chalk dust. Some teachers smell like chocolate-chip cookies. Some teachers smell like Chanel No. 5. I smell like a diesel engine and worse, and when I enter a classroom all the little children chorus, 'Eaow! What's that smell?' and I look accusingly at the teaching assistant. This doesn't actually fool the teaching assistant."

"So who is going to clean the bilge?" John asked.

"It's the responsibility of the captain, my love."

"No it isn't."

"Only an expert can manoeuvre through all the bilge-pump wires, hoses, water-tank overflow pipes and dropped earrings in the bilge. Your trained eye, your clever discernment, your deft hands — they are needed to pump the bilge. My place will be at your side, balancing the hose over the side of the bucket. Wear your orange shorts, my darling. I don't like them, and the pump may splash a bit."

A rare and wonderful feature of the *Inuksuk* is that the bilge water is mostly fresh — if bilge water can ever be said to be fresh. Our bilges are full of escaped drinking water. Well, it was drinking water once, but the dark alchemy of the bilges has transformed it into something dreadful. We do not watch horror films, John and I. When we want excitement, we examine the bilges.

That afternoon found us crouched together in the bottom of the boat. "Heaven spare us," I exclaimed, aiming the flashlight over John's shoulder. "What on earth is that?"

"I wouldn't look too closely," John said.

"How does sludge get in the bottom, and what's that scum on top? Are we growing things down there?"

"Horrible things," John said.

"And that smell!"

"Maybe it's aliens."

"Very funny, darling. I bet we're cultivating a new kind of bacteria, though."

"Probably the plague," John said. "Do we have to do this?"

"Yes, my darling," I said firmly, aiming the pump hose into a recycled lard bucket.

John pumped hard. "How come I'm doing the scut work?" he asked.

"I'm the morale officer, darling, and it's my duty to tell you you're doing a wonderful job."

The bucket filled once — twice — three times, and John dragged it up the companionway hatch and threw the contents into the sea. I crouched over the bilge and sniffed. "Needs disinfectant, darling," I said. "Smells ugly." I handed John a toilet brush and a spray bottle of cleaning potion. "Here."

"You want me to clean the head?"

"I want you to clean the bilge, darling. Scrub with this."

John scrubbed as hard as he had pumped. After a while I sloshed water down the bilge and slopped a little with the brush, then took a turn pumping. The bilge still looked loathsome, but the odour was bearable.

John's orange thrift-store shorts were wet. I'd lain in wait around corners for those shorts for years. My natural cunning was now enhanced by the fumes of old roach bait, disinfectant and mould swirling around my head, and I seized the moment. "Darling," I said casually, "our clothes are filthy. Give me your shorts and shirt and I'll dispose of them."

"Dispose?" John asked suspiciously. "What do you mean by 'dispose'? These are my favourite shorts."

"And I'll see they get a decent burial, my love," I said.

"You can't have them," John said. "I like them. They're perfectly good shorts. Ed the Bald helped me pick them out at Value Village 15 years ago."

"Ed the Bald has all the fashion instincts of a dumpster-diver, my darling," I said, "and I love you, but so do you." I knew I'd lost again, and the shorts would have to wait for something unarguable — like battery acid. Paint, grease and bilge-slime had not dimmed their hypnotic hold on my husband's affections.

We showered, then I lit the candles in the candelabra in the main saloon. "Look, darling," I said, "the flames are healthy — not like the time we boiled all the batteries and there was no oxygen left to breathe with or burn candles — and nothing's exploding, so we really must have cleaned the bilge." I was as happy as the time we had enough cash to hire an exterminator, or the time John agreed in theory — contingent upon money — that refrigeration is a good thing. Some women demand the social rewards that come from the right parties or exotic vacations or a tasteful wardrobe. I will settle for the good opinion of the next teacher's assistant I meet, and little children saying, 'Gee, teacher, you smell nice.'"

Message in a Bottle — The Movie Revisited

"W<small>HAT A BEAUTY</small>," John said. "What a beauty!"

"Do you mean Robin Wright Penn?" I asked.

"No, I mean the boat," John said.

"They've got way too much canvas up and they're heeled over too far," I said. "I bet they're sliding to leeward."

"One Power Squadron course and you're an expert," said John.

I continued. "And look at the desultory way Kevin Costner works on that boat! The marine carpenters I know have thick beards and greasy coveralls. He takes too much time out to shave and do laundry. Just look at the four woodshavings caught on his sweater. Yah! What a dilettante! And he can't make up his mind about anything. The marine carpenters I know know their own minds. 'Twelve thousand dollars,' they say, or '$6,000' if you're lucky. Plus tax. And they skipped the part where Robin Wright Penn clung to the mast and started screaming for help when Kevin Costner let the sails luff, and they cut out the bit where she started yelling that it was all his fault. And what stuntmen hauled all the lines to put up those acres of canvas? Any self-respecting crewmember would be face down on the deck gasping out loud and cursing the captain after raising all those sails. She looks far too relaxed. And her jeans are too tight. It takes flexibility at the knee and hip to crawl over a boat deck. Baggy jeans done right are useful — say, for stopping leaks and cleaning up the bilge."

"Robin Wright Penn would never have made it in Hollywood with your wardrobe," John said.

I ignored him. "The clever sailor takes a woman out sailing only after he's sure of her affection," I said. "First date he takes her down to the dock and says, 'This is my boat. Isn't she pretty? Let's go out to dinner, honey.' No woman feels the same about a man after she's served a picnic lunch at a 45-degree angle with the rigging screaming overhead. And what was he doing sailing toward her hometown to sweep her off her feet? He'd have been better off driving. She was bound to die of old age or find another boyfriend before he got there. Our record is one breakdown per four nautical miles, and it takes practice to get as good as we are. If he was any kind of craftsman at all he'd spend his time working, not sailing or mooning over women. Mind you, I have an advantage over Robin Wright Penn — the women in your past weren't wispy paragons of irresistibility. They were mostly wing nuts. Which one of them thought her psychiatrist was a devil-worshipper?"

"Don't remind me," said John.

"And didn't she set fire to your bed?"

"It was another bed," said John. "Change the subject, please."

"Tell me, darling, do you ever feel the need to keep a shrine to me onboard the *Inuksuk*? Kevin Costner kept a shrine to his wife."

"You have left your own imprint on my life," said John. "That pile of used underwear, for example, but I don't feel the need to keep it."

"Darling," I said, "do you love me enough to jump into the sea?"

"Don't have to," said John.

"Do you love me enough to write love letters and put them in a bottle?"

"Don't want to," John said, "when I can walk right across the main saloon and say, 'I love you' and plant a smacker on your forehead. Now what's for dinner? Fire up the propane stovetop and cook something."

"Darling!" I exclaimed. "Now I know for sure you love me! You trust me with a lighter!" I kissed him. "True love is so much better than in the movies!"

Tools for the Job

ALL WAS SILENT onboard the *Inuksuk*. John was in the engine room, and I was anxiously poised in the passageway. "Do you want anything?" I ventured.

His answer was a grunt followed by a low "Nooo." The grunt sounded contemplative — definitely contemplative. There was another pause.

"How are you doing, darling?" I asked brightly. I peered past the swinging light into the engine room.

"Don't ask," John said. He was hunched miserably in the dark recess on the far side of the engine, looking sombrely at our hot-water tank — our hot-water tank that had gallantly pumped out hot water for the last 20 years and had recently sprung a warm and expensive leak. John had determined that the old tank was beyond repair, so we had bought a shiny new stainless-steel one, and this was the day we planned to pull the old and install the new. The switch had to be swift and complete — we had showers planned for that evening. I smacked my lips in gloating anticipation of all that hot water. Of course, John would have to do all the work, but I had a kind of wordless faith that he would be successful. It was our unspoken division of labour. John did the actual chore while I expressed faith in his ability and handed him tools. This system had worked as reliably as a bilge pump for four years.

"So how's the old one look?" I asked.

"Awful," was the prompt reply. "It looks like toxic waste."

"Can you get it out?"

"I'm afraid to touch it," he said. "But I think so." He grunted softly as he shifted his position. "Hand me a screwdriver," he said.

"Sure," I said. "The blue one, the yellow one or the red one?"

"The Phillips," said John.

"Give me a hint," I said. "Is it big or little or the one with the screw-on handle with all the pointy parts in it?"

"It's the big one," John said.

"Why didn't you say so?" I asked, passing a screwdriver into the engine room. "For future reference, it's the yellow one." There was no reply.

After a while, John spoke up again. "You can take the screwdriver back," he said.

"You mean the yellow one?" I asked.

"Yes," he said, and handed it back to me. "Can you pass me a large open socket wrench?"

"What's it look like?" I asked.

"It's a wrench with an open end," he said.

"What's a wrench?" I asked.

"It's silver, it's big, and it's not a hammer or a screwdriver," he said.

"Where is it?" I asked.

"It should be in the large tool kit," John replied.

"Top or bottom shelf?" I asked.

"Probably the bottom."

I rummaged for a minute. "Is it shiny all over and kind of heavy?" I asked.

"That's probably it," he replied. "And a pipe wrench."

"What's wrong with the other one?"

"Nothing. I need a pipe wrench, too."

"What's it look like?"

"It has a red handle and flexible jaws."

"What are flexible jaws?"

"It has a red handle."

"Okay."

I passed the tools into the engine room.

"Now I need some of those plastic ties, please."

"What do they look like?" I asked. "And why do you need them to take out a hot-water tank?"

"I'm holding up hoses," John explained patiently, "and they're little flexible plastic strips with serrated edges."

"What colour are they?" I asked.

"White. They're in a little brown paper bag."

I passed a raggedy brown bag into the engine room.

"Now I need scissors," he said.

"You're going to snip the tank out of there?" I asked.

"No. I'm going to trim the ties," he said. There was no sound but John's breathing for a minute. Then he passed the ties, scissors and wrench back to me. There was another pause. I peered into the engine room. "It's free," John said. "And the warm water is drained into the bilge. Now we have to figure out how to get it over the engine."

Fortunately, there was some scrap lumber on the dock. From the tangle of stuff I carefully selected a wide flat piece that would balance on the top of the engine. With a little manoeuvring we positioned the board, then John gave a great heave and pushed the heater onto the edge. As the hot-water heater loomed at me out of the dark, a horrified exclamation dropped from my lips.

"My sweater!" I yelled. "My pants!" I grabbed the hot-water tank. "My manicure!" I pulled it through. Large rusty chunks sprayed in all directions. I clasped the rapidly disintegrating tank to my bosom and struggled up the companionway, leaving pieces of tank and rusty footprints behind me. As I dumped the heap into the cockpit, it occurred to me that preventive maintenance was not my beloved's forte, and that if Environment Canada ever caught wind of us we'd be at least charged, if not jailed, for owning such an eyesore. Our hot-water heater in the cockpit was the nautical equivalent of a burned-out car wreck in a front yard. Respectability is my instinct, and I wanted to hide the evidence; I was ready to stop all work and haul the hulk to the dump, but there was a protest from the engine room.

"You're not going to leave me!" John said. "It's dark in here. Be reasonable and pass me the new hot-water heater."

The new heater, by contrast, was shiny stainless steel and rust-free. It was a little smaller than the original heater and it went in easily. I made a magnificent sideways spinal twist, and the heater lurched over the engine. I lay draped over the engine room entrance, festooned with rust, sweaty and bad-tempered. "I need a shower," I said grumpily.

"You may be a little premature," John said thoughtfully. "I have to figure out how to hook this up."

"Does it look complicated?"

"Kind of," John said. "Pass me a hammer."

I sat up suddenly and banged my head on the overhang. "A hammer! Darling, even I know you don't install a hot-water heater with a hammer."

"Nonetheless," said John, "I'd like a hammer. And the yellow screwdriver. The corner of this tank got bumped, and I need to attach hoses."

"What colour hammer do you want?" I said.

For the rest of the afternoon I flipped the switches John asked me to and answered the phone, quite at my leisure. The atmospheric tension in the engine room, however, had increased measurably, and the barometer had dropped in the main saloon in sympathetic understanding.

"Thanks, but I don't think Mr. Dook wants to buy any insurance," I told one caller. There was a thud and the sound of swearing from the engine room. "Do you, darling?" I called.

"Do what?" John asked.

"Want insurance?" I called back.

"No, thank you," John said. I admired the steely control in his voice. "I want hot water. I want a shower. I want to get out of this cursed engine room."

"You've been hunched in there like Quasimodo for most of the afternoon," I observed.

"I know," John moaned. "Would you flip that breaker for me? I do believe we're done." He crawled out of the engine room, looking dishevelled and grouchy. Half an hour later, he poked his head out of the shower. Steam enveloped his round, blissful face. "Hand me some soap, please," he said.

I smiled. "What colour do you want?" I asked.

After all, a man needs the right tool for the job.

Course Crazy

"I'D LIKE TO take a course or two this year," I told John.

"What for?" John asked. "Haven't you taken enough courses?"

"Not at all," I said. "I've taken the basic Power Squadron course, and I've joined the coast guard auxiliary and studied a little first aid and some search and rescue, but I'd like to take some other courses too."

"Judging from the amount of makeup you have in the head locker, you should maybe take a WHMIS [Workplace Hazardous Materials Information System] course next," John said. "Every woman who uses makeup should know about hazardous materials."

"Very funny," I said. "WHMIS doesn't apply at all."

"Of course it does," said John.

"Well, maybe," I said. "But if the stuff at the bottom has deteriorated into hazardous sludge, it's your fault."

"Why is it my fault?" John asked.

"The head locker drips," I said.

"It's condensation," said John.

"'Tisn't."

"'Tis."

"'Tisn't."

"'Tis."

"WHMIS would be a useful course to take before cleaning out the food locker in the main saloon."

"Why?"

"The food locker drips," I said. "It's your fault."

"It's condensation," said John.

"'Tisn't."

"'Tis."

"'Tisn't."

"'Tis."

"Or WHMIS would be good to navigate my way through the musty stuff in my clothing locker," I said.

"It's condensation," said John.

"'Tisn't."

"'Tis."

"'Tisn't."

"'Tis."

"Maybe I could take Foodsafe," I said, "seeing as how we've been refrigeratorless for nearly three years now."

"Sarcasm won't chill the milk," John said.

"Neither will the galley lockers," I said. "We need a new refrigerator."

"The Vikings sailed without refrigeration," said John.

"You see any Vikings around Cowichan Bay?" I asked.

"Well, no," said John.

"They all died of food poisoning," I said, "and so will we if I don't get some freon gas. Tell you what. You take Foodsafe and I'll take a sailing course."

"Doesn't the coast guard auxiliary give you enough excitement?"

"I guess it does," I said.

I had joined out of a sudden surge of patriotism. The average terrorist, I reasoned, would be properly frightened by the sight of a peri-menopausal woman wearing orange and bearing down on him in a coast guard auxiliary boat. Every Thursday night I put on my popsicle-coloured cruiser suit, jam a toque on my head, gloves on my fingers and leaky sneakers on my feet and look for imaginary floating debris with a spotlight.

"The west coast is safe now that I've joined the coast guard auxiliary," I said. "I personally rescued a fender last Thursday, and I've spotted about a hundred crab pots and jellyfish. I know every crab pot between here and Cape Keppel and I've named some of the larger jellyfish after local personalities — Naval John, Screaming Liver, Ed the Bald, Older-Than-Dirt Don and Stafford the Respectable."

"Such a pity you weren't as expert at finding the dinghy we lost in Georgia Strait," John said.

"That was before I joined the auxiliary," I said. "I wear popsicle orange as a symbol of mourning for that dinghy and the spotlight I wave is like an eternal flame in its memory. Every time I go out on a coast guard exercise I mentally salute our gallant little dinghy, shot at by the American navy in Whiskey Golf."

"So were we, as I recall," said John. "They were firing torpedoes that day, but they weren't armed with warheads so it hardly counts."

"You see? You see? Courses are awfully useful things to take. Why, if I'd been paying attention during that Power Squadron course instead of drinking coffee and telling funny stories, I never would have gotten us into that situation. Foodsafe, and we'll never be doubled over with botulism. First Aid, and I'll save your life just in case my canning fails. WHMIS? I'll spray Simple Green and roach spray around like an expert, and dispose of tainted canned goods without poisoning the shellfish clinging to the bottom of the boat, and a sailing course is self-evident."

John sighed. "Marriage," he said, "my last decision. You make a persuasive argument in favour of taking courses. It all sounds so attractive, but promise me one thing."

"What?"

"If you're going to take a sailing course, pay attention during the man overboard drills."

"Whatever you say, my Bilge Water Baby," I said. "I wonder if I can find a course on survival cooking?"

Men in Orange

W E MEET ON boats — me and the men in orange. I'm a member of the Cowichan Bay Coast Guard Auxiliary. I'm brave and intrepid. Sometimes I'm all wet. Our boat is the *Excalibur*, a beautiful powerboat that slides along at eight knots, carrying loyal auxiliary members and spotlights, first aid supplies, a generator, a back board, water hoses, and extra life jackets. The other coast guard auxiliary has faster boats — rubber dinghies with sleek lines and big, powerful engines and flashing GPSs. They all have crash helmets because their boats go fast. They all have neat stuff hanging off their orange cruiser suits. I'm jealous of the other coast guard auxiliary. I tell myself they're no better than we are — they just have nicer stuff and can go faster.

John and I of the Cowichan Bay Coast Guard Auxiliary enjoy going to meetings. We've been known to have beer after meetings. William, a new member with wild enthusiasms and a loud voice, often calls aloud for a beverage during exercises, but we have rules about giving William beer. Beer might excite him too much. William is young and exuberant and waves his searchlight wildly to annoy the team leader. The team leader makes speeches about the importance of our exercises out on the water. William asks if he can have a beverage. The team leader tells us it is necessary to be serious. William says he seriously wants a beverage.

We return to our stations and comb the surface of the dark water looking for flotsam, jetsam or whatever the team leader has thrown overboard for us to find. Someday we may pull a body out of the water, so we practise on fenders and life jackets. I suggest we practise on other people's crab-pot floats and then have boiled crab later, but the team leader gives me the same look he gives William, and I am quenched.

One night, we go on a joint exercise with the other coast guard auxiliary, and the real coast guard. The real coast guard is mean. They set us awkward tasks and ask difficult questions. I am nervous. What if the other coast guard auxiliary does better than we do? But then, a stroke of luck. Our boat is designated on-scene command boat. Our team leader can tell the other coast guard auxiliary what to do. He tells them to set up an expanding square search pattern in the middle of the chart. They spend the exercise revving their engines and spraying foam, dashing at incredible speeds around and around, their teeth bared and their crash helmets gleaming in the moonlight.

The other coast guard auxiliary is good at navigation and stuff. Every now and then they radio us. "Sitrep," they bark into the receiver, and give us co-ordinates. "Sitrep" means "Situation Report." It gives me chills when they use abbreviations. When I am on the radio, I don't know what to do with the co-ordinates.

"That's nice," I say, "er ... thanks. Uh ... Roger. Carry on." Our team leader can't always be at the helm. He has to keep track of six boats and tell William and me what to do. And how to do it. He is always polite, though we know his instinct is to throw us overboard. William and I like our team leader. He does not give in to his instincts.

Suddenly, someone spots the dinghy we are looking for. Luckily, it is our team. I feel smug. Our team leader calls all the boats together. The other team leader leaps gracefully onboard our boat, the *Excalibur*. "Here are the parameters of our search," he says to our team leader, "in case you want to mark them on your chart." In the cabin, I make a convulsive movement with my hands to hide our chart. I was in charge of recording. There is nothing marked on our chart. I and William of the Cowichan Bay Coast Guard Auxiliary have superior abilities. We keep stuff in our heads.

We hang out on the deck of the real coast guard boat for a while, then we go home. The seas are safe, thanks to me and the men in orange.

We are chilled through. The subdivision of Arbutus Ridge nestled on Vancouver Island, twinkles at us, and the motors throb. The sky is dark and deep and the water is wet and cold and black — black as sin. There are no stars.

We saved another imaginary life tonight. We spotted a dinghy and called the skipper's name in the dark. He was not there, but he wasn't drowned either, just uninvented when the exercise ended, and we are going home to our beds, sated with cold oxygen and adventure. Our feet are like ice cubes and our fingertips are chilled.

I learned something tonight. A sector search is best if you're sure of your datum, and the fast rubber boats should do the shoreline searches. I almost felt like one of the guys — unwieldy, but not unwelcome. I stood on the deck of the coast guard boat with the other rescuers, one of the few times I've ever fit in wearing that shade of orange.

It's dark and cold, and my flashlight casts a thin glow across my paper.

I will stop now, and sit, and enjoy the vibration under my feet, the warmth of the cabin, the feeling of having accomplished something, and the tiredness that creeps across my neck and shoulders.

Roger that.

Excalibur out.

Excitement on the Docks

IT WAS A typical Cowichan Bay afternoon. Out on the bay lay a collection of pretty boats at anchor — all visitors. At dock lay a motley collection of local boats — ferrocement, fibreglass over wood and untended plyboard, most with blue tarps stretched over the booms in anticipation of the decks leaking during the next rain. Buddy the cat crouched by an electric meter midway down the dock. Power cords, telephone wires and water lines lay tangled down its length. It was low tide and the rusty ramp rose sharply to the cement pierhead next to the fish market.

It was on this pierhead that, when substitute teaching was slow, I once slit the gills of a thousand salmon for Tony, the mad fishmonger.

When I showed off my visiting grandson, Mikey, to Tony, I bragged that "he gets his brains from granny."

Tony replied, "Surely the little fellow can do better than that."

The dark Hallowe'en night I caught most of Tony's staff painting his forklift pastel pink, I swore I'd never name names. I think it was the forklift that did it. Tony left the fishmarket forever to go back to fishing. He said he felt the need to kill things.

After Tony left, there was never any excitement on the pierhead at the top of the dock. Until today. This was the day John and I were testing the propane oven we had bought cheap at Boater's Exchange.

John stood poised over the stove, lighter ready for action. The stove, a three-burner, stainless-steel Finnish model with an oven and real thermocouples, sat between us. I don't know what thermocouples are, but Steve at Boater's Exchange told us they're good things, so I'd been telling everyone "AND thermocouples," and they'd all looked impressed.

The stove was attached by a length of hose and a regulator to a small white propane tank that had been loaned to us by Ed the Bald and filled up with propane by John that morning.

I stood anxiously to one side clutching a fire extinguisher. Ed himself, standing well back, broke the silence. "Needs cleaning," he said. "I have some stainless steel cleaner in storage. And you shouldn't have bought a new regulator. I have two somewhere."

"You have everything in storage a body could need plus four vacuum cleaners," I said. "Ed, you're amazing."

"Quiet," said John, twisting knobs. "I'm listening for propane." He flicked his lighter on the first burner. Nothing happened. The second — the third — the oven. Nothing. "Now what?" asked John.

German Bob came up the ramp. "Hey, Bob," yelled Ed the Bald, "do goose-steppers know anything about propane?"

"Propane? Ah! A new stove! Sure," said German Bob. He knelt and began twisting the same knobs John had.

"We have thermocouples," I said, pointing proudly to the little grey metal rods sticking up from the burners.

"Thermocouples!" he exclaimed. "Why, there's your problem! You have to heat the thermocouples to bleed air out of the line. Where's 'on'?" He twisted all the knobs on the stove, pulled out a book of matches and began lighting and dropping them on the nearest thermocouple.

Jean-Paul happened by. "New stove?" he asked. "It don't work? Maybe you got no propane." He lifted the tank and shook it. "Empty!" he said. "Well, there's one way to test it." He fiddled with the regulator and pulled it off the tank. A hiss of propane hit the air. German Bob dropped another lit match.

"Quit with the matches," I exclaimed. "There's propane!"

"I can't bleed the line if you're going to unhook it!" German Bob yelled at Jean-Paul.

"You don't know much about propane! Hah!" Jean-Paul yelled back.

Ed the Bald slid sideways and disappeared. John looked confused. "Perhaps we could eliminate one possibility at a time," he began.

"We got thermocouples," I interrupted. German Bob threw down the last of his matches and left.

Gary, the marina owner, came by. "New stove!" he said. "So that's what all the excitement's about!" He waved one hand, in which was a lit cigarette. I aimed the fire extinguisher at it.

"We got thermocouples," I said.

"Thermocouples don't make no difference," said Jean-Paul, screwing the regulator back into the tank and turning the stove on its side. He fiddled with the knobs and flicked a lighter. Gary left, casting a nervous look at my fire extinguisher. Jean-Paul, fierce and intent, leaned over the oven.

You know, he figured it out. Turns out you have to press the knob in and hold it while you light the burners. To bypass the thermocouples.

Yes, we miss Tony at Cowichan Bay. But as long as we are let loose with second-hand appliances and propane bottles, we shall try to duplicate the adrenalin rush that he gave us. I can almost hear his voice.

"Tony — we got thermocouples."

"And I got ex-wives. Bite me!"

Cleaning Up

"W E NEED TO clean out our storage unit," John said.
I gasped out loud. "There's valuable stuff in there," I said.
"It's full of junk we never use."
"I know it's there," I said.
Cowichan Bay storage units are a valuable part of the liveaboard
life. The liveaboard clings to his storage unit like a drowning man
clutching a passing piece of flotsam. It may not save him, but it's
deeply meaningful — at least for a while. My neighbour has a
season's worth of jam in hers. Naval John stores his collection of
cell phones and barber tools left over from World War II. Jean-
Paul and Endis own a collection of offshore gear, well-used and
bleached white by the Pacific sun. I happen to know that Ed the
Bald keeps 300 plastic coat hangers in his, and I own a bicycle
held together with rust patches, teaching materials up to my
armpits, Christmas presents I couldn't find last year in time for
Christmas ... the rest is a kind of black hole that sucks stuff into
its gullet and never releases it.

John and I stood in front of the doorway to our storage unit. "Gird
your loins, my little dumpling," he said. "What must be done must
be done."

Ed the Bald passed by on his way up to the road with his dog, Joey.
"Let me know if you throw anything out," he said. "I get first crack
at it." Ed is a pack rat of even greater ability than I.

"It will do me good to know my things have gone to a good home," I said.

John rubbed his hands together. "At last — a good clean-out," he said. Reluctantly I pressed the tiny key into our padlock. The lock sprang open and the dusty wooden gate swung heavily to one side. I took a deep breath as I peered into the dark, dripping recesses of our unit.

"Look at all that wonderful stuff," I said.

"I bet there's spiders in there," John said.

Bravely I took a step forward. I picked up a coarse brown duffel bag from on top of my bicycle and heaved it onto the floor.

"We can throw out these old sails," I said. "We never use them."

"What?" John spluttered. "Once we recut them, they'll be fine."

"And this old radio," I said enthusiastically.

"Maybe we can fix that radio," said John stubbornly.

"And look at these blocks of foam — we'll never use them. Let's toss them."

"Cushions," John said weakly.

"And these old batteries — what are they good for?"

"We can recharge them — they'll be good spares," John said.

"This paint — no good," I said firmly.

"It matches the boat," John said feebly.

"And these roller brushes — they're just taking up room."

"We paint the boat every year," John said piteously.

I dusted my palms together. "There, I'm done," I said brightly.

"What?" John exclaimed. "You want to throw out all my good stuff. What about your stuff? Look at these two trunks of teaching materials! You haven't touched them in four years."

I threw myself in front of the trunks. "Someday between now and retirement, I may get a full-time job again, and I'll need all my tapes of Inuit music and Dolch vocabulary knock-offs on a pirate theme for primary English-as-a-second-language aboriginal students. I generated those vocabulary sheets myself."

"The title didn't sound mass-produced," John agreed.

"And those beautiful pictures of Ski-Doos and endangered Arctic animals, and the words to 'Jesus Loves Me' in Innuanaqtun, the book of international string games and kamik boot patterns, a pang hat crochet pattern — I may need them again."

"You'll never find them in those trunks," John said reasonably. He sighed. "Oh, all right. What's in this suitcase?"

"Books," I said.

"Books? They're no use in storage."

"You're right, darling. Let's move them onboard."

"Perhaps not," John said. "Leave them here. What's in this box?"

"Important videos, my sweet."

He picked up a case. "*Peter Pan*. Aren't you a little old for cartoons?"

"Now John — didn't you always want to run away to sea?" I said. John pointed to the breadmaker. "You never use this."

"Of course not, darling. Our power cord can't suck amps that hard. But someday we'll own a little shack in the woods, and maybe when we're feeling reckless you can fire up the generator and I'll make bread with my breadmaker by the light of our one 40-watt bulb."

"Pioneer women made bread from scratch," he said.

"Pioneer women were dead by my age — probably from baking too much bread from scratch."

We stopped and looked at each other. We had not mutually agreed to discard anything. My face brightened as I spotted something. "Look, John — a plastic hanger! We don't need this, do we?"

"No," John said, pleased.

"I'll give it to Ed the Bald," I said, "to add to his collection. I think we're done, darling, don't you?"

"I guess so," said John. We locked up the storage room door and walked back down the dock toward the *Inuksuk*. The plastic hanger hung jauntily from my hand.

"A good morning's work, wouldn't you say, darling? You were absolutely right. That storage unit really did need cleaning out."

Norman the Navigator

A TRIM GREEN sloop, tiny and perfect, lay moored in a slip next to our neighbours' boat. "Pretty boat," said John. "I wonder who owns her."

The companionway cover slid back and a head popped through the opening. "Ahoy this ship," I said.

The owner of the head flashed a grin at me. "You live here?" he asked.

"We do," said John. "I'm John. This is my wife, Catherine."

"Norman," he said, emerging from the depths of his little sloop. "I don't live aboard, but I'll be here a lot."

We at Cowichan Bay rely on a complicated system of observation, speculation and invention to analyze each other. For example, when an attractive woman we'd never seen before left a note at the door of Stafford the Respectable's floathome and then fled furtively up the ramp, we felt duty-bound to glance at it. Not to read the contents, you understand — we're not nosey — but we wanted to do a quick handwriting analysis to determine if her character was of a sufficient standard for our friend and neighbour. Stage two was an interview with Stafford to glean further information, and the tertiary stage was an analysis of the interview with my neighbour, who segued into the disclosure that Stafford keeps mice in his freezer to feed his pet snake. "Pet snake!" I gasped. "Snake!"

"Mice!" said my neighbour. "He's a really nice guy, and he let me keep my groceries in his fridge the day I was locked out of my boat, but mice! My groceries were in the same fridge as dead mice!"

"Biologists are not all that marketable," I said. "We should be grateful anyone dates him at all."

Naturally, once we found out that Stafford the Respectable owned dead vermin and a snake, we felt honour-bound to let everyone know.

But back to Norman. As soon as his boat arrived, there was wild speculation as to his character, habits, proclivities, income and marital status.

"Nice little boat," said Screaming Liver. "Keeps it up. And he goes out in it a lot."

"Pleasant guy," said Ed the Bald.

"I think he's a lawyer," said my husband. "He should be able to afford boat parts."

"But he wants to quit and go sailing," I said.

"Divorced or separated. He has a girlfriend. She's really friendly," said my neighbour.

"Fibreglass boat," said Fred. "He's having problems with his transmission, though."

"Not a bad sailor," said Jean-Paul.

"I haven't met him," said Stafford the Respectable, with a reproachful look at me. "You didn't have to tell EVERYONE I keep a snake."

"He gave me bubble gum," said Angelique. "He sails to Bubble Gum Island."

"He's getting really good at docking," said my neighbour. "And he goes out in all weathers."

"I still haven't talked to him," said Stafford the Respectable. "Lots of people keep mice in their freezers."

We all tried to be on hand to catch lines whenever he docked so we could pump him for information. He went out often and never reported getting lost. We began to call him "Norman the Navigator." He sailed in fine weather and inclement, returning from one successful sail after another with only a moderate amount of mechanical dysfunction. His lady friend never showed signs of shock upon their return. We know because we scrutinized her closely for symptoms of what we at Cowichan Bay refer to as "The Dook Syndrome."

"How come," asked my neighbour, "Norman the Navigator spends quality time sailing when the rest of us are in our slips repairing our boats? We don't even have an engine."

"We're having our engine rewired," I said. "Ed the Bald is saving up for a starter, Jean-Paul is fibreglassing his head, Screaming Liver sprang a major leak last week, and Stafford the Respectable has to work so much he hardly gets out in his kayak."

"But he's still having trouble with his transmission," said Fred. "He should see Bob — now there's a guy who knows transmissions."

"He shouldn't go out in fog," said John. "Dangerous."

"I wonder how his girlfriend puts up with his heavy-weather sailing," I said, "but she doesn't seem to mind."

"Any girlfriend of mine will have to like the same things I do," remarked Stafford the Respectable.

"You've got dead mice. I'd say your chances aren't good," said my neighbour.

Public opinion had turned against Norman the Navigator. To a person, we seethed with jealousy.

Then one evening we saw his boat limp home in the dark. He was single-handing, and he was on his second attempt to back into his slip. "My reverse is shot," he yelled across the few feet of water. He looked disgusted and exhausted. He made another ragged approach. "I had trouble the whole trip," he complained. "My transmission is gone and I'm flat out of money to fix it." He passed his stern line to John, picked up his bow line, stepped off the boat, slipped on the edge of the dock and fell straight into the ocean.

With a shout Fred jumped to help him up. We exclaimed and tied lines and commiserated. He stood on the dock dripping and laughing. He was wet and broke and his boat was busted.

"Welcome to Cowichan Bay, Norman," I said. "We love you."

Head Aches

JOHN CAME INTO the main saloon from the head. "Darling," I said, "isn't life wonderful? Here we are on our little boat, snug and happy. Even though we're broke, I have the day off today and we can spend it sipping apple cider and listening to CDs. Come here and give me a kiss. I think you're terrific."

John didn't say anything.

"John! What's wrong?" He was silent. "Tell me it isn't true! Tell me it's not the head!"

John sighed. "It *is* the head. Doesn't work." I blanched. I rely on the head like my Irish ancestors did the bottle, and an abrupt cessation of access is apt to bring on acute symptoms, like the crawling DTs. My life flashed in front of my eyes.

The first facility of my youth was a chemical toilet in the unheated back porch of a duplex in Churchill, Manitoba, on the shores of Hudson Bay. The toilet seat was perched on top of a honey bucket streaked with condensation. In the icy cold, by the light of a naked light bulb with a string hanging from it, in a room with rough lumber walls, I would balance one knee on the toilet seat, hold my breath, duck my head down the hole while I swung myself up, and clamber onto the seat. Short people climbing onto tall chemical toilets couldn't skip the head-partway-down-the-hole step.

Mom prided herself on being first of the neighbourhood ladies to dump the honey bucket into the cesspit every single morning. Of such subtleties were the hierarchy of Arctic society built 40 years ago. I have childhood memories of Mom in her gumboots, scarf and parka opening the outside door at dawn to a shrieking wind with fistfuls of snow in it, struggling to haul a full honey bucket into the weather. I never heard her complain.

This admirable role modelling did not, as it might have, inspire me to rush headlong into graceful young womanhood and all the benefits of marriage and family. So in Grade One, when Donald Duff proposed marriage, I turned him down flat.

When I was seven, we visited my grandparents in the south. It was then that I was introduced to my first flush toilet. The shiny porcelain, the gleaming chrome handle, the great roar of the flush and above all, the way it smelled, left me delirious with joy. I flushed five or six times in a row to watch the water spin away, entranced, until my mother made me stop.

During that same visit my grandfather sat me on his lap and said, "Catherine, if you want to catch a husband, you have to act a little stupid." I thought this was hilariously good advice, so when in Grade Five Calvin Westwood tried to kiss me, I blackened his left eye. Violence was considered equivalent to cleverness on northern Manitoba schoolyards in the 1960s. I didn't want a husband. I knew his parents had a chemical toilet, just like ours, and I wasn't going to be trapped into a relationship with a lad who didn't have the kind of plumbing for which I yearned.

Years later I found myself in Kugluktuk, Nunavut, surrounded by shiny bathroom fixtures, a toilet with a foot pedal, a water-holding tank, a complicated sewage-disposal system and a roommate named Skinner who was young enough to be my son. Many of the teachers roomed together to save money. Skinner was a Maritimer and an excellent math teacher, but a lousy haircutter, which service he would perform only after being pleaded with and plied with beer. Skinner spent his spare time jigging for cod down a six-foot-deep ice hole with his fingers frozen to a jigger, leaving me to polish the toilet bowl and organize toilet paper.

Then I fell in love with John at the school board office. I'd had one of those years from hell where you want to quit teaching and go into turnip farming, and John was the board executive who was detailed to entertain me with little photocopying jobs just before the superintendent of schools turfed me out, forever, at the end of my contract. John was so sympathetic I married him. When I found out my destiny was true love and a 44-foot ketch, I naturally asked about the plumbing.

"You shall have an electric head, my dear," John said, and I fell ecstatically into his arms. He neglected to mention I'd have to help him fix it when it broke down. But I married John for better or for worse, and as a major stakeholder in the ongoing drama of the head, I felt obliged to contribute.

I dug the rubber gloves out of the locker by the sink and held them out. "Here, darling," I said.

Five hours later the head had been taken apart, cleaned, primed and reassembled. John had struggled with the screws and tested all the impellers, kneeling on the floor in an inch of questionable water. I had held the flashlight. When the job was done, John pressed the electric starter button. With a boisterous roar, the macerator churned madly, but not one drop of water entered the toilet bowl. "It's running dry — there's no water intake!" John's voice was anguished.

A dry sob caught in my throat. "No water intake," I echoed. John set about pulling the head to pieces again.

Later, we looked at the electric motor with narrowed eyes. "Intake here — arrow — outlet," John said.

"Let's test it," I said. "Let's hook it up with a hose and a pot of water and make sure it's sucking."

"Good idea," said John.

We crowded into the head with my favourite Tupperware bowl, the electric motor and a length of flexible plastic hosepipe. I stuck the hosepipe into the water while John connected the wires, and I braced myself for the spray out the opposite end when he pressed the button. There was none. Instead, great gulping mouthfuls of air glugged into the bowl. Feverishly John tore the hose off the pump, connected it to the outlet and pressed the starter button. Water raced through the pump and sprayed onto the wall. John's finger dropped from the button. We stared at the pump.

I cleared my throat slightly. "Darling," I said, "I am not really clever at this sort of thing, but the water is travelling in the outlet, out the inlet and in the opposite direction to the arrow. This pump is pumping in reverse."

"That's impossible," said John. "The head worked before."

"But not well," I argued. "And as soon as you primed the impeller, it was sealed up tight and now it pumps water better than it ever did — in reverse. It sort of worked before because the impeller was still going around — in reverse — and the blades were grabbing little bladesful of salt water to send in the wrong direction, and there was a vacuum created by the action of the impeller, sucking a little water even though it didn't want to go there. Remember we took the motor apart because the impeller wasn't doing its job? Now, what's the only thing that would make an electric motor run in reverse?" I looked at the arrow again. "Switched wires, darling. Switch the wires."

"You may be right," said John. "It's worth a try." He switched the wires, inserted the "in" nozzle into the pot of water and pressed the starter button. The deluge of water from the "out" nozzle shot clean across the head and soaked us both.

"It works!" I gasped, too overcome with emotion to yell out loud. "It works, darling."

"It's not supposed to," John said. "How come it worked before?" He attached the electric motor to the head. "It's been hooked up that way for a year. It worked before. How come?" He knelt to attach the head to the floor and hook up the hoses. "It was pumping in some water, and it was pumping out just fine." He connected the wires. He pressed the starter motor. The head filled with water and swirled down toward the macerator.

"Voila," I said. "You may notice that now there's lots of water. Before there wasn't enough."

"How'd you get to be so smart?" John asked.

"Well, darling," I said, "do you remember when we were courting?"

"Of course," said John.

"Well, I may have acted a little stupid," I sighed contentedly. "But now that I've got a real husband and an electric head of my own, I don't have to. Isn't this wonderful, darling? A cosy boat, a working head and time to ourselves. Come here and give me a kiss. I think you're terrific."

The Children Came on Two by Two, Hurrah!

A THIN BEAM of sunlight pierced the damp air to illuminate the aft cabin.

"Wake up, John," I said. "Lisa's coming to visit today!"

John groaned. "How many children does she have again?"

"Darling, Lisa is our daughter. Her three children are our grandchildren. Their names are Jessica, Douglas and Mikey. They all get their brains from Granny. I suppose technically I'm a step-granny, but I'm the one who sends birthday money, so that makes me Granny. They're very clever children, and they reflect well on me. Only a very rude grandparent forgets his grandchildren."

"Only a very foolish grandparent invites three of them onboard a boat." He looked reproachfully at me. "This is all your fault. And which of us gets to drive to Nanaimo to pick everyone up from the ferry?"

"Why, you, darling," I said brightly. "I have to stay here to tend to Paul."

"It's raining," he said flatly.

"Why, so it is," I said. "Drive safely, darling."

"Seven people on our boat," he grumbled. "We'll be as crowded as the ark. How big are they now?"

"Jessica's 13, Douglas is 10 and Mikey is nearly 2 — and Paul is 23 and six foot three."

He moaned and turned over. "There's too many of them and they're too large."

Later Paul was up and medicated. "Mom!" he said. "Hi hi Dad!" Then he settled happily into his morning toast and coffee, and stretched himself out on the settee berth in the main saloon in front of the TV.

"Daddy John's going to get Lisa and her children," I told Paul.

"Bad baby," he said, and laughed delightedly.

"He remembers Mikey," I said to John happily. "Isn't that wonderful?"

"He remembers how Mikey climbed the settee berth and threw books," said John. "And the time he chewed on the parachute flare."

I laughed lightly. "Such a precocious child. He gets his brains from his granny."

"Bad baby," Paul said again.

"I agree with you completely, Paul," said John.

Later John arrived with our visitors. The children tumbled down the companionway, waving gym bags and packsacks. I screamed out loud in delight and threw myself at the foot of the ladder to catch and kiss them as they landed. "Douglas!" I screeched. "It's Granny! Jessica! You're so beautiful! Mikey! Give Granny a kiss! Lisa! You look exhausted! Sit down! Who'd like something to eat?"

John stood in the cockpit in the rain. His face was contemplative and gentle — as if his mind had transported him to a quiet place where there were no intruders. He made no move to climb into the main saloon. His hair flattened a little in the rain. "Come down, darling," I said.

"I think I'll just stand out here for a while," he said softly. "I wonder how Noah coped. It rained for him too, didn't it? How many animals did he fit on the ark?"

Inside the main saloon, I served coffee to the adults and milk and cookies to the grandchildren. Jessica and Douglas sat stiffly on a settee berth and nibbled cookies and glanced politely around the saloon. Paul sat up and looked eagerly at the children. Lisa lay back and closed her eyes. Mikey cannoned from one berth to another, waving cookies, spilling milk and yelling with the sheer joy of living. All five of us watched him — me smilingly, Paul happily, Jessica and Douglas interestedly and Lisa fondly. John climbed down the companionway and sat beside Paul. With a howl of delight Mikey ran full tilt toward the companionway, climbed the ladder and was chewing on the ignition key before I could lunge in his direction. All three adults yelled simultaneously, then I caught myself and turned to Lisa. "Fast little guy, isn't he?" I said weakly. "He gets his brains from Granny."

Lisa dragged a yelling Mikey off the ladder and handed him to Douglas.

"Take care of your brother. Mikey adores Douglas," she said serenely.

"Come on, Mikey," Douglas said. "Let's go in here," and they disappeared toward the aft cabin. We all sagged a little into our seats. There was relative quiet in the main saloon.

I smiled at Jessica. "Tell me, dear," I said, "what would you like for Christmas?"

"Oh, I don't know," she said composedly.

"What do you think Douglas would like?"

"Socks and underwear," she replied without hesitation.

There was a yell from the aft cabin.

"Douglas!" Lisa yelled. "If you're going to fool around on that bed, take your shoes off!"

"Okay, Mom," Douglas hollered, and we heard two thuds as he threw his shoes.

"And Mikey's shoes too," Lisa yelled. A pause, then two smaller thuds.

Jessica folded her hands and settled them primly in her lap. "He likes boxer shorts," she said.

"Pokemon cards?" I ventured. "Harry Potter?"

"He likes boxer shorts best," she said. "Knitted. And socks." Such out-and-out treachery left me stunned for a moment, then I glowed with pride.

"A little sibling rivalry, I think. She gets her brains from Granny," I said.

There was a crash from the aft cabin.

"Bad baby," Paul said excitedly.

"Quit that, Mikey," Douglas yelled.

"Douglas, what's going on in there?" Lisa said.

"Nothing, Mom. Mikey, quit that!"

John stood up. "I think I'll go stand in the cockpit for a while," he said.

"But darling, it's raining," I said.

"Oh, I don't mind a little rain," he said, "when you consider the alternative. How long did it rain on the ark?" He climbed the ladder.

"So how was your trip over?" I asked Lisa.

"Just wonderful," she said. "The kids were angels."

"Mommy, Mommy, Mikey's fallen on the engine and I can't find him!"

"Why not?" Lisa called.

"It's dark," Douglas said.

"I don't hear any splashing," I said, running toward the engine room. I leaned into the passageway and felt around the engine, pulling Mikey to safety. "You're a good babysitter," I told Douglas. "You get your brains from Granny."

Mikey slipped past us, dropped on all fours and dug for the broom, ripping it out of its corner. Then he careened wildly down the main saloon toward the head, chewing on the bristles and swinging the handle. We ducked in unison. Douglas raced after him.

"Bad baby," Paul said.

Jessica smiled subtly. "Definitely boxer shorts," she said. "White." Douglas caught up with Mikey at the head. There was a clunk as the broom handle smacked into the door.

"Mikey! Stop that!" he yelled.

"He likes polka dots too," Jessica said calmly.

Douglas and Mikey raced through the main saloon in the opposite direction, the broom handle dragging behind Mikey. Lisa grabbed the broom and removed it firmly from Mikey's grasp. Mikey opened his mouth into a large O and shrieked. Lisa dug into a canvas bag and pulled out a small toy.

"Minnie Mouse," she said, and waved it in front of Mikey, who grabbed at the toy and stuffed it into his mouth. Then he climbed onto the settee berth and reached eagerly for a pair of binoculars. They slid onto the cushions, just as John came back.

"He likes white socks too," Jessica said.

"So how long will you stay?" John asked Lisa.

"Three days," Lisa said. John blanched. "But I thought we'd check into a hotel, Daddy." John and I beamed happily.

Mikey leaned over and bit Douglas. Douglas yelled in pain.

"Bad baby," Paul said.

I smiled fondly. "You get your brains from your mother, Paul."

The Bible doesn't tell us how Noah and his wife coped with the animals for 40 days and 40 nights. Some of them were no doubt better behaved than others. Did they quarrel? Did they run amok through the main saloon? Did they spill their food and rampage through the aft cabin? Did they trip over the oars and interrupt conversations? This I do know: the minute there was sun, Noah leaned out of the ark, released a little bird and begged it to come back with an olive branch. Or the address of a hotel.

Renaissance Man with a Scalpel

JOHN CLIMBED DOWN the companionway waving a small plastic parcel filled with medical paraphernalia. His face alight, he kissed me happily. "Look what I got!" he said. "It was a terrific presentation."

"So now you know all about first aid at sea?" I said. "Well, I'm glad you had a good time."

"I know how to use a catheter," he said. "Can I practise on you? I have a nice catheter in this packet. Never been used."

"And let's keep it that way, darling," I said. "When I was a kid, we used to operate on Mr. Potato Head. That was before the days of plastic potato heads, and we used real potatoes. Potatoes were so expensive in the Arctic, Mom used to recycle them for supper."

"You had *potatoes?*" John exclaimed. "We had to use rocks!"

"You had *rocks?*" I said. "Sometimes we had to use gallstones."

"Speaking of gallstones," John began.

"You lost that round. Admit it, darling," I said.

"We had to recycle our gallstones for rocks," John said.

"You win, my love," I said.

"I met Ed the Bald coming down the dock, and I offered to operate on his gallstones."

"And did he jump at the offer?"

"Well, no. He showed me his sore finger, so I volunteered to amputate. I was just getting the scalpel out of my packet when he said he had to walk Joey. Do you need anything sutured?"

"Those sail covers, darling."

John ignored me. "I wonder how Fred is feeling," he said.

"Now, darling," I said, "I always said you needed a hobby, but this is as bad as the time you decided to take up home dentistry."

"I have all the tools," John grumbled.

"No, darling," I said. "There are limits to what even I would let my own true love to do my teeth. And there are laws against practising medicine without a licence."

"At sea the captain is in charge," John said. "Besides, extraordinary situations call for extraordinary measures. Did I ever tell you about my most exciting flight with a half-crazed Arctic bush pilot?"

"No, darling. I'm all ears," I said, pulling out my peeler and digging in a galley locker for potatoes. I ran water into the sink and began peeling. "Tell me what happened."

"He was flying me to Cambridge Bay in a Single Otter one spring. I was the only passenger. During takeoff one of the skis flipped up and got caught in the rigging. We couldn't land with the ski up, of course, so he cracked open a side window in the cockpit, pulled out a rifle, leaned out the window and began firing at the rigging."

I dropped the potato I was peeling and stared at John. "My glory! What happened?"

"Well, luckily he was a good shot. He hit the wire that had tangled up the ski, the ski flipped back into position and we landed smoothly as a figure skater. He's crazy, but he is my hero."

"Give me those sutures," I said firmly, reaching to snatch the package of medical supplies out of John's hand.

"They're mine," he said, holding the package out of my reach. "And you never know what might happen at sea. Did I ever tell you about the time I went into the hospital in Fort Smith to get a chest X-ray and came out with a dislocated finger?"

"You expect those sorts of things to happen in Fort Smith," I said.

"Or the time I dislocated my shoulder climbing over a wall in Spence Bay 30 years ago? My loyal staff bundled me into the Co-op

Bombardier to take me to the nursing station in the middle of a blizzard. Unfortunately, they'd been working on the engine that day and they'd left the engine cover off. The engine on a Bombardier is between the driver and the passenger and my pants caught on fire, so I arrived at the nursing station with a dislocated shoulder and on fire. We extinguished my pants, and a burly nurse drugged me and wrestled with my shoulder for a while, until she gave up. She decided to keep me drugged until the blizzard blew out and they could medevac me to Cambridge Bay. It took three days. On the third day someone put me on the back of a Ski-Doo and raced me to the airport. Halfway there I fell off and the driver didn't notice. The fuel truck crew saw me face down in a snowbank, picked me up and delivered me to the airport. The fuel truck crew worked for me. It always pays to treat your staff well," John said reflectively.

"I can hardly wait to go offshore with you, my darling," I said. "What happened then?"

"Well, we got to Cambridge Bay, and a doctor popped my shoulder back into place in less than a minute. I was so heavily drugged, I didn't care one way or another. It was quite an adventure."

I finished peeling the last potato and began to rinse them. "You really have done everything, haven't you, my love?" I said.

"Except operate," John said. "I've never operated on anyone."

"Well, darling, you've practised on Mr. Potato Head. Practise on these potatoes now, and cut them up for me — there's a dear. We'll leave more adventurous medical experiments for real emergencies. After all, there's nothing wrong with either of us. You won't give up your scalpel? No? Let's visit our neighbours after supper. I wonder how Fred is feeling?"

Beauty is in the Eye

"THIS ISN'T AN easy ways, like the other one," John said, "so be careful."

I turned a little pale. The last ways had been perfectly awful, and I had been in a state of perpetual terror the whole time the boat had been balanced on what looked like a fragile matchstick or two and a rickety railing. John, Jean-Paul and Ed the Bald had put the boat on the ways this year while I was at work, and I was hurrying down the street toward the new ways with my purse clutched nervously under one arm. I was wearing a ground-sweeping skirt and sensible shoes, perfect for chasing primary schoolchildren across a playground. I shivered and pulled my sweater closer. The sun had set and it was suppertime. I was hungry. John, always considerate, had met me at the car to escort me home. This year we were hauling out in the fall; our last haulout had been in early spring, and we were concerned about our zincs.

"Did you make supper, my darling?" I asked.

"Wieners à la propane as soon as we get on the boat," he said. "And beans."

"What a catch you are, my love," I said. So clever of John to entice me up the ladder with hot food. My standards in food change when someone else offers to cook. I don't feel the same passion for vegetables, or the same need to inflict Canada's Food Rules on the man I love, who hates everything except beans.

We strode down the street arm in arm past the Starfish Studio and the fish market, closed and dark, past the old Cow Bay Café with newspapers covering the windows and past Bayside Video, lit up and cheery. Bayside Video awakens and stretches just as everyone else on the strip curls twice and goes to sleep. "Let's poke our heads in the door and say hi to Bill," I said.

"You're putting off climbing the ladder," John said. "Come on — wieners await you."

We hastened down the wooden sidewalk and then stopped in front of the ways. John gestured confidently. "Here she is," he said. The *Inuksuk* loomed out of the dark, crouched between two tall, ramshackle buildings, as massive and inert as the Sphinx.

"My," I said weakly, "it's dark, isn't it?"

"I have a flashlight," John said.

"Do you have a bucket onboard?"

"I have a bucket."

"Are the water tanks full?"

"The water tanks are full. The captain is prepared for anything. Stop stalling."

I draped my purse around my neck and descended the steep wooden stairs to the ground. Huge greasy beams lay across the ways, and waist-high cables. Gravel and shellfish crunched under my sturdy shoes. John's flashlight beam danced across the bow of the *Inuksuk*, then caught a glimmer of orangey-brown bottom paint on the hull.

"Did you paint?"

"Didn't have to," John said. "The bottom was nearly clean. Beautiful, isn't it?" He stopped and played the beam of the flashlight over the hull. I started to laugh. "What's so funny?"

"If anyone had ever told me that one day I would be standing on top of dead shellfish, up to my knees in dark, admiring the bottom of a boat by flashlight, I never would have believed it. The things we do for men!"

When I taught on the reserve, I was expected to stand around a deer which was in the advanced stages of rigor mortis and exclaim joyously that the hunter had killed it with one shot. In the Arctic, I was expected to stand around a Ski-Doo and shout over the roar of the motor that it had started well — on only the fifth pull. But when my Kugluktuk roommate caught his first Arctic char and kissed it ecstatically on its little frozen lips, I offered to introduce him to some girls. Men have peculiar passions, and polite female admiration seems to be a necessary adjunct. Seeing beauty through the eyes of a man is a learned skill. As I stood on the ways in the chilly dark with my purse slung around my neck, I felt as though I was on the brink of a great truth — as though within my reach was wisdom far beyond that of my immature self who at 20 had once said, "Corvette, shmorvette!" Male Corvette owners are testy about ridicule.

"It *is* beautiful, darling," I said. "Lucky we won't have to paint this year." The thin flashlight beam lit up a slender ladder propped almost vertically against the starboard side of the boat. I gasped out loud. "A ladder! Darling, you mean I don't have to be hoisted 20 feet in the air by a halyard?"

"Sarcasm will get you nowhere," John said. "Who's first?"

I reached out to touch the silvered, paint-bespeckled wood of the ladder. It trembled.

"Me," I said. "You can catch my 20-stone body as it comes hurtling down."

"I'd be killed instantly," John said, "so don't fall. I'll aim the flashlight up the ladder. You'll be fine. Hold the hem of your skirt in your teeth so you don't trip on it."

"Is anyone looking?" I asked.

"Only me," said John, "and we're married." I stuffed a mouthful of hem into my mouth and cautiously began my ascent. The ladder shook slightly. Hunching my shoulders and attempting to flatten myself against the rungs, I took one step up the shaking ladder, then another. It was easy in the dark because I couldn't see enough to terrify myself, and with my mouth full of skirt, I was too preoccupied with hanging on by my teeth to yell out loud. I landed on the deck of the boat and crawled on my hands and knees toward the companionway entrance.

"What a system!" I exclaimed as John clambered onboard after me. "Except for the tooth marks on my skirt, climbing up the ladder in the dark is the best way to do it. I'm hardly terrified at all." I looked brightly around me. "Can't see a thing." I climbed down the companionway, slid slightly aft and then righted myself. The main saloon looked comfortable as a hug. John climbed down the companionway and flipped on the 12-volt light in the galley. I sighed with gratitude. "Home safe and slanted," I said. "Bucket positioned for action, tanks full and wieners ready to be propaned — life is wonderful."

When I admired the deer, the man wasn't mine so I didn't have to butcher it. When I admired the Ski-Doo, the man wasn't mine so I didn't have to ride it. When I admired the frozen char, the man wasn't mine so I didn't have to thaw and fillet it. This year, even though I was married to my wonderful John, I didn't have to paint the hull I'd admired so much — just climb it. Perhaps that was why, for the instant I stood in the dark exclaiming over the hull, it really, truly did look beautiful.

Thrift-Store Madness

THE OTHER DAY I came home in a heightened state of delight, and climbed backwards down the companionway, swinging a ragged plastic bag from one hand. "Look at this!" I exclaimed. "Kiss me quick and look what I found at the thrift store!" I threw my coat into the forward cabin. John, settled in a corner of the settee berth, didn't move. He looked unimpressed and vaguely uncomfortable — as if I was blocking the TV while Valerie Pringle was saying something important. Reverently, like a magician drawing treasures out of a hat, I drew a brightly coloured stack of plastic cups out of the bag. "Tupperware, darling," I said. "Twenty-five cents apiece."

"What are we going to use those for?" John asked.

"For drinking juice out of, and water," I said. "And rum."

"Rum is good," John said.

"Whatever you say, my sweet," I said. "Look at this." I waved a beige sweater through the air.

"What's that for?" John asked.

"To wear, darling," I said. "I can wear it while I'm driving the car, teaching school and buying bottles of rum."

"It looks pretty nice," John said. "What else have you got?"

I pulled out a white teddy bear with a red ribbon around its neck. "Only $3.99, darling. I know our adorable little grandson Mikey would be thrilled to know Granny saved enough on his Christmas present to buy his grandpa a bottle of something nice."

"And did you?" John asked.

"Well, no," I said, "but I spent 25 cents on this 40-year-old paperback on dating."

"You're married to me," John said. "Why do you need a book on dating?"

"You own an old Corvette," I told him. "Why do you need a babe magnet when you've already got the babe? For fun, of course. We can lovingly share passages about dating over a drink of rum."

"No, we can't," John said. "You know we don't have a drop of liquor onboard. You haven't let me buy any since the December before last."

"That is a lie from start to finish," I said. "We have at least an inch left of the gin we use for killing fish and half a litre of cooking wine, finest quality. Would you like a Tupperware cup of anything, darling?"

"I think I'll settle for water," he said morosely. "A sailor, drinking water — imagine!"

"We could put some Pepsi and nutmeg in the gin and pretend it's grog."

"No, thank you." John said hastily. "Water will be fine." I poured water into two pumpkin-orange cups, slipped on the sweater, then curled into the opposite corner next to the teddy bear with my new book. John sipped his water, while I raced eagerly through the pages of *Datebook's Complete Guide to Dating*. When I got to the chapter "Active Sports Dates," my neighbour popped her head into the main saloon.

"Listen to this," I said excitedly. "This is the advice they were giving teenage girls in 1963. 'If you are hurt, lie quietly and calmly while your date gets aid. He'll feel terrible; don't make it worse. No hysterics, no dramatics — it's all part of the game.'"

"Sounds sensible to me," John said.

"Can you imagine the poor girl lying there with a broken arm, whispering, 'Don't mind me — just drag me to one side and play around my body.' "

My neighbour hooted joyfully. "Fred would have taken the advice

134

literally," she said, climbing down. "Don't let Fred read that book. Fred, don't read that book," she called up the companionway to Fred, who was on the deck. I continued reading aloud.

"'This is definitely not the time to put on an exhibition or give him a lesson, no matter how good you are. If you show off and show him up, you'll strike out permanently.'" By this time my neighbour and I were helpless with laughter.

John sat with a slightly puzzled look on his face. "What's wrong with that?" he asked.

"'And no matter what your score, you will win if he makes another date. Bear in mind that you are playing a more important game than the one being scored, and act accordingly. Your date, of course, is unaware of the Big Game.'"

"Is there a Big Game?" John asked.

"There *is* a Big Game, John, and we lost," said Fred, who then climbed down the companionway after his wife. "Have you been thrift-storing again, Catherine? Don't show my wife your teddy bear."

"Oh, isn't he cute!" my neighbour cried.

"Like my sweater?" I asked. "$5.99."

"Looks good on you," she said. "You did well."

"And look at these," I said, flourishing the little cups. "Tupperware. Cheap."

"No!" she gasped. "Real Tupperware?"

I filled the last two cups with water and passed them to our visitors.

Fred looked over at John. John looked at Fred. "Real sailors drink rum," John grumbled.

"Wife won't let me have any either," said Fred.

"We could have done worse," John said. "Imelda Marcos, for example."

"Nancy Reagan," said Fred.

"When we won the Big Game, we both did well too." I said to my neighbour. Silently we toasted each other with Tupperware.

Mutiny Among the Mates

THE WOMEN OF Cowichan Bay are a brave lot of nautical pioneers who keep up appearances. Oh, we may look happy — swilling coffee and chopping chives gleaned from our deck boxes, pausing while swabbing bird droppings off the deck to pass on gossip, and exchanging cheery greetings while hauling five-gallon containers of diesel fuel in our little wheelbarrows, but it's all a façade to hide our dark side. Every now and then, we whisper mutiny in quiet corners, while our husbands start their engines. Camouflaged by great choking clouds of white diesel exhaust, we quietly compare notes.

I have observed, in private, to my neighbour that my nerves are not what they used to be. A marine mechanic once told my husband that an electrician should look at our electrical system. I believe he used the words "dog's breakfast." Naively, I awaited the day my dear husband would hire an electrician. I have waited four and a half years. In that period we've had two explosions, two melted plugs and a fire when a light fixture melted. But that doesn't count. John explained it all to me. That particular socket was always a problem, he said, because it always was hot. I believe I said, "Oh, that's all right then, darling. The socket was hot. Now I feel completely reassured. Come here and give me a kiss. You're so clever." I may be paraphrasing.

Judy, quietly and serenely, has mentioned that she is mildly irritated by her Murray's reluctance to let her use the fire extinguisher. Her definition of "fire" differs from that of the man she loves, and she has elaborated on two-foot flames roaring in the engine room, and the domestic disagreement that ensued. Murray won and the fire was extinguished with drinking water, but Judy remains vaguely petulant over not having had her way.

With a sigh Anne has told us of voyages with Blaine. All of them, she says, ended with the kind of mechanical failure that tends to ruin the pleasure of the trip. Her melodious voice trembles a little as she speaks of the time their transmission blew up. She inhales a little exhaust, and she coughs.

My neighbour has told us — not complaining, you understand, but just mentioning in the course of a conversation — that their boat has been without an engine for upwards of five years. She mentions it to Fred every now and then, but she says he doesn't appear to notice.

Marilyn went a year and a half without hot water. This did not seem to inconvenience Geoff, so the situation was never rectified and Marilyn washed dishes, did laundry and bathed, all with the aid of a small kettle and a propane stovetop.

We once complained as a group that our husbands often got lost while driving. "Did Jean-Paul ever get lost in the Pacific?" we asked Endis.

"Oh yes," she said softly. "Lots."

But the queen of suffering at Cowichan Bay remains forever imprinted on our psyches: the woman who went a year without a marine toilet. I write of Shirley. Craig, she explained, choking on the diesel exhaust as she spoke, has a prejudice against putting holes in the hull. He was completely content to use a bucket, until one day she explained that she was on the verge of leaving forever to live out her life somewhere — anywhere — there was plumbing. We were stricken into silence.

There is much we women of the docks are willing to endure to be with our husbands. But quietly, subversively, the first mates at Cowichan Bay are beginning to organize. Let the next man who starts his engine at the dock look to his crew.

A Picture is Worth a Thousand Words

UNDERSTANDING COMES SLOWLY to those of us who live afloat — like osmosis. I learn about things by hanging around the Bluenose Restaurant and listening to John, John and Jim. Yes, for the cost of a cup of coffee (plus tax) I can listen in on some of the most enlightened, informed conversations you could hope to find anywhere. The only problem is interpreting what they say. Jim, for example, is a mechanical genius whose speeches are nearly unintelligible to anyone below the rank of engineer. However, when John (not my husband — the other one) interprets, I am able to comprehend a little more. Then my husband John draws a diagram on a paper napkin with the pen he keeps in his breast pocket, and understanding gushes upon me like seawater through a broken seacock. Because I am the lowest filter on the cheesecloth of understanding, the men do not always get as far as me, and I sit sipping coffee and knitting socks in a kind of polite fog, a look of interested enquiry frozen on my visage. Conversation over coffee is the Cowichan Bay winter activity of choice.

"The drinking water in Genoa Bay is no good," said Other John.

"No wonder. You should see the set-up they have there," said Jim.

"The water in Cowichan Bay gives Catherine a stomachache," said my husband.

"There's iron in it, and enough trace minerals to cause upset in some people, but the regular bacteriological analysis done by the water inspectors proves it's safe to drink," said Jim.

"Or at least that's what they say," said Other John.

My husband pulled out his pen. "Let me draw you a picture of the filtration system," he said to me.

"Darling," I said, "draw me a picture of a bacterium — say an E. coli, with little legs."

"Oh, all right," said John.

"What are your plans for the day?" Other John asked Jim.

"I'm still working on that engine," said Jim. "The tensile strength of the metals I've got on hand are incompatible with the valves of the pistons I've got."

Other John turned to my husband. "Causes wear. Can't mess around with incompatible metals."

"I'll draw you a diagram of a gas engine," John said to me. I pulled a knitting needle from behind my ear and picked up six stitches on the heel of my sock.

"Oh no, darling. Draw me a picture of a car — say a Volkswagen."

"Oh, all right," John said. He turned to a passing waitress. "Jill, can we have some more napkins, please? We're running low here."

As Jill passed a handful of napkins to John, she bestowed on me an intelligent look of sympathetic understanding.

"Are the boys ripping engines apart again?" she asked.

"Still," I said, and we grinned at each other.

"Some idiot worked on those heads before I got to them," said Jim.

"You have to get the measurements exact to a very fine degree — thousandths of a millimetre," said Other John.

"Here's a head from a diesel engine," John said, busily drawing.

"Oh, isn't that cute?" I said. "Draw a face on it, darling — and ears."

"I nearly joined the British Sports Car Enthusiasts' Club years ago," said Other John, "until I started talking to some guy who told me he owned an Austin-Healey 3000."

Jim and my husband laughed incredulously.

"Overweight," Jim said.

"Underpowered," Other John said.

"No style," my husband said. I looked politely from one to the other and continued knitting.

"What colour was it?" I asked. John and Jim turned expressionless faces toward me.

"Here, let me draw you a picture," my husband said hastily.

"Of an Englishman with a bowler hat on a motorcycle, darling," I said. "Oh, how lovely."

My neighbour and her husband Fred came into the restaurant and sat down at our table. "Buenos dias," said Fred. "Habla English?"

"Habla français?" I asked.

"Habla Inuktitut?" John asked.

"Socks again?" said my neighbour to me. "Pretty nice."

"So how's life, Fred?" asked my husband.

"My computer crashed yesterday, and I had to reload all my programs for my website," he said. "I have three Windows 98 second-generation programs running in different compartments, so I can boot every one up separately. Easy."

"Fred!" my neighbour exclaimed. "What on earth are you talking about?" She turned to me. "Do you know what he's talking about?"

"Well, no," I said. "John darling, draw us a picture of a computer — there's a dear."

"Don't know anything about computers," John said.

"Me either," said Other John.

"Me either," said Jim. Everyone looked uneasy. Then Jim's face cleared. "Fred," he said, "have you solved that problem with your car yet? Looks like it was leaking when you had it parked."

"I think it's one of the connections," Fred said.

"If it's overheating, you're losing radiator fluid somewhere," Jim said.

"The fluid in the radiator cools the engine, so if you leak fluid your engine overheats," Other John explained.

"Let me draw you a diagram of a radiator," my husband said.

"Oh no, John," my neighbour said. "Draw us a picture of some water instead. We like water better, don't we, Catherine?"

"Speaking of water," said Other John, "have you heard that the water at Genoa Bay is undrinkable?"

Bacteria Bob

Just the other day the *Inuksuk* had a distinguished private visitor in the person of "Bacteria Bob," a public health inspector for one of the Canadian Arctic territories which I will not name for fear of a libel suit. Bacteria was happily drinking coffee with us in the main saloon when he elected to be given the whole 64-cent (American) tour of the boat. I showed him all the cunning beauties of the *Inuksuk* and had just flung open the door to the head when I realized to my horror that for reasons completely beyond my comprehension, John had stored a pot of covered raw crab on the shelf there. To his credit, Bacteria maintained perfect composure, but I did notice that he declined an invitation to eat crab with us.

As I watched our visitor beat a hasty retreat up the companionway, I was reminded of my youth in Churchill, Manitoba, and the town waterman who delivered water once a week to the water barrels on our back porch. Fifty years ago the public school curriculum in Manitoba didn't "cover" germs until Grade Four. Since the waterman had formal schooling only up until Grade Three, he didn't believe in germs. This was a tremendous advantage to him in his choice of profession.

Each time the public health inspectors from Winnipeg condemned his truck, he'd proclaim that he "didn't believe" in germs, and nothing anybody could say would change his mind. What he did believe, just as passionately, was that the Liberal government was responsible for the public health inspectors, so he voted Conservative with fervour. The week Diefenbaker was elected happened to coincide with the scheduled visit of the health inspectors, who, true to their yearly ritual, condemned his truck again and then returned to Winnipeg.

The poor man was considerably downcast. "I'm gonna vote NDP," he told my mother morosely, "but I ain't got no faith no more. Them political bastards, they all stick together."

Every now and then he'd consent to have the town pay to have his truck cleaned, but usually a public health nurse followed behind him, explaining how to sterilize drinking water.

I would have felt as though I had risen above my childhood (which I was lucky to survive, the Arctic considered) had Bacteria Bob consented to eat a meal with us. Snobbery in the North is based on oddities one doesn't usually consider in the South.

Come back, Bacteria Bob! For you I will spray bleach around like water. For you I will throw the raw crab into the sea. For you I will make John install refrigeration. What am I saying? I should count myself lucky that the man I love doesn't see a menacing swarm of pestilence in my galley, doesn't notice that I've gained 50 pounds since I married him, and eats canned beans with relish the suppertimes I'm too tired to peel potatoes.

Politics, hygiene and the love of a good man: Cowichan Bay is a regular hotbed of passions. Yet still I yearn to have my housekeeping blessed by the best. We may look grotty and sleepy and have homemade haircuts, but we have souls like other Canadians. Come back, Bacteria Bob!

The Destiny of the Dooks

"J OHN JR. IS returning soon with his intended bride," I said. "You should sit down with him and have one of those father-son talks."

"Son, there's this stork ..." John said.

"Darling," I said, "you have five children and you never figured out where they come from?"

"The stork was a frequent visitor at our house," John said thoughtfully. "Louise went away every now and then, and she'd come back with a baby. She picked out nice ones. Lisa was the first. I had to put bars across the top of her crib to keep her from crawling out in the middle of the night and wrecking the kitchen."

"Two years old and a convict?" I asked.

"She grew out of it," John said. "Maggie was always losing her diapers. When she was a baby, she had all the instincts of a stripper. Then there was Jackie. We nearly lost her once."

"No!"

"She was born in England, and when we came back to Canada she was eight and Immigration wouldn't let her in. She stood on the other side of the immigration barrier weeping big tears while we argued with the officials. They finally gave her back to us, though. The time we lost Rupert, we were on holiday. We left him at a gas station. Could've happened to anyone. Rupert wasn't bothered. He was just about to ask the mechanic to adopt him, when to his disappointment we came back and took him away from the garage. Rupert always was interested in machinery. John Jr. likes machines too, and he dresses like a man who has just finished fixing something. He had a little suit when he was five. He sure looked handsome. Nobody's ever been able to dress him up since."

"Well, darling," I said, "there's going to be a wedding. Do you think his new bride will be able to wrestle him into a suit?"

"Were you able to wrestle me into a suit?" John asked.

"Yes, but not since the nuptials, darling," I said. "Paul is my contribution to the family, and he wears whatever I knit for him, bless his heart. When he was little, what an escape artist he was — he saw a horizon and he dove for it — just like his step-daddy." I pinched John's cheek. "Are we going offshore because you adore adventure, or because you're escaping all our children?"

"Both," John said.

"But what if the stork follows us offshore?" I argued. "After all, you don't know much about the habits of storks, but they seem to like you."

John turned pale. "Why don't they take one baby back when they deliver the next one — like beer bottles?" he asked. "If you got pregnant, I'd send everybody out for ice cream, and then I'd cast off the mooring lines and sail away."

"How gallant, my darling. But the problem with Dooks is that they're irresistible to the opposite sex, and the next thing you know, there's more Dooks — by marriage, birth or adoption. The stork is the Dook destiny, my love."

"I want a bigger boat," John said.

"The other thing you have to explain to John Jr. is that the Dook who is irresistible to the opposite sex, and who is a stork magnet, has to live with the boat length he can afford."

"Oh," John said.

"I'm glad you're going to have this talk with John Jr., darling. Paul is my baby, and Rupert has left a trail of repaired machines and broken hearts all over the Arctic, but John Jr. has found the right woman, and you must explain his fate to him."

"Irresistible attraction, stork, short boat." John sighed. "By the way, John's fiancée has a little girl."

"It's happened already!" I gasped. "It's the Dook destiny!"

Survival: *Inuksuk*

Dᴀʏ 10, Cᴀᴍᴇʀᴀ 1 — Main Saloon

I sat in grim silence, my chin sunk on my chest, my lower lip thrust out and my forehead furrowed in a scowl. John approached me timidly. "Are you all right?" he asked.

"Not all right," I said. "Why don't they move out?"

"They haven't got any money," John said reasonably. "Besides, John Jr. is related to us by reason of his mother having given birth to him."

My voice lowered to a snarl. "They've been living with us for ten days on a 44-foot boat. After ten days in a space this small, white rats gnaw each others' legs off. I'm at the leg-chewing stage now. I love our daughter-in-law Lisa, our new little granddaughter Alix is wonderful and John Jr. used to be the apple of my eye, but that was eight days ago. Now I want to murder him and bury his body at sea. Children over the age of 30 shouldn't live with their parents. It's not natural."

John sighed and patted my shoulder. "Maybe they'll leave soon," he said. We both gazed painfully into the middle distance.

Day 11, Camera 2 — Forward Cabin

Daughter-in-law Lisa stirred and poked John Jr. "John!" she whispered. "Wake up!"

"I wasn't asleep," he murmured. "Can't sleep. These cushions are too thin and this bed is as hard as a rock."

"I haven't had a decent night's sleep since we got here," said Lisa, "and Catherine snores like a steam engine. And her cooking! I haven't swallowed that much lard since the last time I had a week-long binge of happy fries. I think I was 13. And one more crack about my parenting, and I'll throw her overboard. There isn't a jury of daughters-in-law in this country that'll hang me for it."

"Dad has always been terrific to me," said John Jr., "but he won't let me use his car, and how am I supposed to fix my truck so I can work if I can't get where the truck is? As for Catherine, she's just crabby. Try to get some sleep. I wish we had some money."

Day 13, Camera 3 — On the Deck of the *Inuksuk*

Alix and her neighbour Angelique were playing on the deck of the boat. Angelique turned to Alix. "Let's ask your granny for some cookie," she said. "Your granny is Catherine, right?"

"Granny always says no," said Alix sadly. "She gives me crackers and milk instead. I wish I had a treat."

"Catherine used to be nice," said Angelique, "last week. Your grandpa is John, right? Let's ask him if we can play with the wheel until the lights go on on that panel-thing."

"Grandpa used to be nice too," said Alix. "Maybe if I ask Granny for some bread crusts to feed the seagulls we can eat them instead. I dropped a nickel in the toilet yesterday and Granny's mad at me."

"I dropped my gum in their head last year and Catherine laughed and said little girls do silly things," said Angelique, "and then your grandpa patted me on the shoulder and said visit anytime."

"Maybe they like you better than they like me," said Alix. "I wish I had my own room. And a puppy. Granny snores, you know. Let's catch some jellyfish."

Day 14, Camera 4 — Aft Cabin

John and I lay snuggled in bed. I sobbed quietly while John patted my back. "Take that pillow out of your mouth, Catherine, and tell me what's wrong."

"I used to be so happy," I hiccuped. "Hap-hap-happy. I was a mother of six, and they had all moved away. Far away. John Jr. went to Bella

Bella. Jackie's in Nunavut, Maggie's in Yellowknife, Paul's in Edmonton, Lisa's in Vancouver and nobody knows where Rupert is but when he visits he stays in ho-ho-hotels. Rupert is my favourite child."

"Every parent looks forward to the day when his children leave home," John said sadly.

"Yes," I said, sitting up in bed and eagerly grasping his arm. "But the baby books never tell you that they come back — like malaria — and that enough visits can kill you — like dengue fever. I used to be so maternal," I continued. "Everyone said so. I'm starting to understand the lab rat who eats her young — she too just wants to be first at the head."

Camera faded as I went hysterical and had to be sedated with gin.

Day 15, Camera 1 — Main Saloon

Alix sat directly in front of the TV. All four adults were crowded on the two settee berths. Cartoons careened loudly across the TV screen. Alix looked absorbed. Nobody spoke, made eye contact or smiled.

Day 16, Camera 3 — On the Deck of the *Inuksuk*

John Jr. and Lisa sat in the cockpit. John and I sat on the deck. Alix played on the dock, fishing for fingerlings. "Dad, Catherine," John Jr. said. "I have a job now, and my truck is fixed. We'll move out tomorrow."

I fell to my knees and offered thanks to Heaven, bruising one leg on a stanchion. John closed his eyes. His lips moved. Lisa beamed. "I went out today and bought some salad for supper tonight, Mom," she said. "You let me take care of cooking. It'll be a celebration."

John Jr. handed his father $20. "Here's some money I owe you," he said.

I embraced him fondly. "I know you'll come up with the other $580 when you can," I said affectionately. "But don't worry about it a bit. We love you. When can you move?"

"First thing in the morning," John Jr. said happily.

"First thing in the morning," I repeated reverently. "Did you hear that, darling? First thing in the morning." I sighed ecstatically. "Do you need any help?"

"We're already packed, Mom," Lisa said. "We can be out of here in ten minutes. Even less."

Alix approached the side of the boat. "Can we go right after breakfast, Mom?" she asked. "Can I have treats? Do we get a refrigerator to put freezies in? We do? I love you, Granny."

Camera faded as family performed a group hug.

Day 17, Camera 1 — Main Saloon

It was afternoon. John and I were sitting on a settee berth. "John Jr. did well to get a job so soon." I said. "He really is a credit to us. And Lisa is a wonderful housekeeper. That little Alix is adorable — so affectionate and well behaved."

"They are a good little family. I'm glad they're doing so well," said John.

I looked around the main saloon. "It's awfully quiet in here," I said wistfully. "I wonder if they'd like to come back for supper."

Close-up shot of John's shocked face.

Cut to credits.

The Mystery of the Bilge

"I KNOW WHAT to get you for Christmas," John said. "A Swiffer."

"A Swiffer?" I said. "Whatever for?"

"Every woman wants a Swiffer," John said. "That's what they say on TV. A Swiffer is the next generation in cleanliness engineering. More than a broom, more than a mop, with its handy handle and scientifically moistened head, it makes cleaning floors a joyous occasion. The women in the ads look as ecstatic as you do when you're eating fudge."

"I'm not sure that TV is the best place to gain an understanding of your wife's mind."

"You can learn a lot from TV," John said. "For example, I know what to get you for our anniversary."

"What?"

"The fifth anniversary is the cheeseburger anniversary — with fries for good behaviour."

"Uh huh," I said. "It's lucky you're cute, because you're not very well behaved."

"And I know what to get you for your birthday."

"And that is ...?"

"Glad garbage bags. The Man from Glad explained it all to me on TV."

"You don't do enough boat maintenance," I said. "You spend far too much time watching TV."

"The TV never explained that boat maintenance was on your mind," John said. "The TV told me you were obsessed with eliminating upholstery odours."

"TV women don't live on boats," I said. "They chase aliens and dust pianos. They're lawyers in slim skirts who eat fast food and admire nature up close from the passenger seat of a van." I snorted scornfully. "The women of Cowichan Bay can't afford to eat out in fancy restaurants like Wendy's. Most of us aren't professionals, none of us have ever worn a slim skirt and we mostly drive beaters as far as Country Grocer. We relate well to strange species, though. I speak of the men of Cowichan Bay. And I'm sure the men of Cowichan Bay say the same of us. But boat maintenance is on my mind, my darling stud muffin," I said. "Solve the water-tank problem."

"Today?" John said.

"Yes."

"'Seinfeld' is coming on next," John said.

"Today."

"And after that, 'Third Rock from the Sun,'" John said.

"Today."

What goes on in the recesses of our bilge? The mystery is a deep and frightening one, and until we can afford a plumber it may remain as impenetrable as the ocean at Cowichan Bay when the bottom is stirred, and as inscrutable as Iron Mike when he's tending his tomatoes.

We have four steel water tanks connected by a valve system that would confuse an engineer, let alone simple folk like John and me. John lifts up a wooden grille on the floor and there the valves are in a row — seven of them — colour-coded for our convenience. The fifth red one, which one's fingers may clutch by accident when reaching for red valve #4 under the slimy floor, will sink the boat, but only if you turn it the wrong way, which is right. I think.

Filling the water tanks takes a skilful hand and a fine ear. You see, no one can actually tell when the tanks are full. Each tank gives its own subtle signal. The starboard wall tank (left yellow valve right,

152

right yellow valve left, first three red valves right and fourth red valve left and don't touch the fifth valve) suddenly goes silent, then lets out a loud "boom." Then you hear the sound of rushing water as the overflow shoots into the bilge amidships, and the bilge alarm dings frantically. John lunges for the fourth red valve and turns it right as fast as he can. "Port wall tank?" I ask tersely. John nods grimly, his face strained. He turns the first red valve left and listens intently. This tank is troublesome, and will boom even while being filled slowly. We listen nervously for the sound of water sliding into the bilge, which is our only warning on this tank. Booming doesn't count. Sometimes we wuss out, and when the booming gets to us, John will nervously twist the valve right. "Floor starboard?" I ask. John nods. Third red valve left, and we listen for the sound of water trickling into the bilge. There is no booming, so we are cautious and turn off the radio. John twists the third red valve right.

"Port floor tank," he says. "Shhhh." This is the smallest and most silent of the tanks. John twists the second red valve left and crouches over the rectangular opening in the floor. The only warning this tank gives is a slight bubbling noise. There — it's full. John twists the second red valve right and jumps to his feet to turn off the water on the dock. Then, climbing back into the main saloon, he turns the left yellow valve left, the right yellow valve right, and the fourth red valve left. This starts us using the starboard wall tank first. Then he opens the tap in the galley and releases a stream of water, judging by the ascending roar of the water-pressure pump when it is best to slap the tap shut and listen for the pump to cut out. It took us a year to perfect this system.

But there is a mystery in the bilge, and we cannot fathom it. At unexpected moments, like in the middle of the night, the water-pressure pump cuts in, indicating a sudden loss of water pressure. Why? At other times, the bilge alarm dings wildly and fresh water pours out the side of the vessel. Why? And sometimes the wall tanks are mysteriously empty and the floor tanks are mysteriously full. Why?

Is there a stranger who comes onboard to take showers while we're out? The wall tanks appear to be siphoning into the floor tanks, and the floor tanks appear to be siphoning into the bilge. Leaking valves? Overflow pipes? Holes in the tanks?

We sat unhappily in the main saloon, our heads spinning and our coffee cooling. I sighed and broke the silence. "Darling," I said.

"Yes?" said John.

"Buy me a Swiffer."

"Whatever you like, my little Snoggy-Lips. Would a Swiffer make you happy?"

"This mystery is beyond our ken. Fate is against us. She who can't solve the mystery of the bilge and whose husband is baffled must settle for less. A Swiffer would make me happy, my darling. Let's see what's on TV."

Let There be Peace on Earth

"LET THERE BE peace on earth, and let it begin with me," I warbled. "Let there be peace on earth, the peace that was meant to ... would somebody shut up that idiot pit bull? She's barking her fool head off!" I was decorating our two-foot Christmas tree in the main saloon and stirring the last of my Christmas fudge. It was early November, but I like to jump-start Christmas before the rush. The air was filled with the scents of diesel and chocolate and cream, and that peculiar happy aroma that comes from a small, damp, plastic Christmas tree that has been stored under a fish market for 11 months. The neighbours' dog had been barking like mad for an hour. Nika started barking every morning and gave full throat for hours. Her owners, who lived onboard the *Shogun*, worked seven days a week in Victoria and were gone from early morning until late at night. "With God as our Father, brothers all are we. Let me walk with my brother in perfect ... I think I'm going to stick my head out the hatch and yell at Nika. Maybe that'll shut her up."

John looked up from his newspaper. "Where's your Christmas spirit?" he asked.

"It doesn't extend to pit bulls," I said grimly. "You know I hate dogs. Ever since I was attacked by a husky at the age of seven, I've hated dogs."

John put down his newspaper. "Nika's never attacked you," he said.

I sighed. "I know I'm not being very Christian about this," I said.

"And if I don't have a handle on 'Love God and love your neighbour,' I've missed the point, but Nika's not my neighbour."

"Then who is your neighbour?" John said, and returned to his newspaper.

I ran to the galley to give my fudge another stir. Who was my neighbour? We were a motley lot down at the docks, but mostly we got along. Older-than-Dirt Don had been a guest in one of Hitler's hotels in the Netherlands at the end of the war, eating potato peelings and nettles for three months until he was liberated by the Canadian army. And didn't he paint German Bob's deck a couple of summers ago? And didn't German Bob check on Older-Than-Dirt Don every day when Older was sick with the flu? And didn't he spend all year walking Ed the Bald's dog, even though he wasn't overly fond of Ed? My neighbour and her husband, Fred, are Jehovah's Witnesses who listen politely while I talk about Christmas. The South Pacific veteran Jean-Paul has one artificial hand but he helped paint our hull during our last haulout. Some of our neighbours have come looking for us when we sailed in the wrong direction, some of them have towed us home when our engine failed us, and when Nika's owners ran the local restaurant they baked John's birthday cake and gave us extra fries every time we asked for fish and chips. Who is my neighbour? I paused to listen to Nika bark.

"I bet that dog is lonely," I said. John didn't say anything. "I bet she'd enjoy a walk every night," I said. John still didn't say anything. "I go for a walk every night with the neighbour lady," I said. "I could take Nika with us."

"Sounds like a plan to me," said John

"My fudge is done and the tree is decorated," I said. "I'm going to see if anybody would like a stroll up the road." I bundled into a sweater and sneakers and headed up the companionway. My neighbour and Nika were both delighted to see me.

We walked along the road from Cowichan Bay every evening for a month, braving rain and wind and fog. We panted and puffed and climbed the hill and slogged past houses and bush and Hecate Park and other dogs. Sometimes Nika and Joey got to touch noses when German Bob was walking Joey. My neighbour and I visited and laughed and exchanged recipes while Nika patiently strode alongside. We became a part of the local scene — two middle-aged ladies and a black pit bull walking down Cowichan Bay Road in the dark. By December, all three of us had trimmed to an attractive girth.

"I've lost ten pounds," I told John, as I wrapped the last of the Harry Potter books for the grandchildren. I snapped some cellophane tape off its dispenser and attached it to a bright parcel. Then I hunted for my scissors in the jumble of scraps and books and socks and pocket knives and CDs. I could hear Nika bark through the hull of our boat.

"It's almost time for our nightly constitutional," I said. I climbed the companionway and stuck my head through the hatch. "Hang on, darling," I yelled. "Auntie's coming!" Joyfully Nika barked in reply. "She hasn't stopped barking a bit," I said, "but she sounds a lot happier."

I began to sing, "Let there be peace on earth ..."

Scarlet Ribbons

I WAS STANDING in the reception area of a muffler shop, a phone stuck on one ear. "John darling," I said into the receiver, "they said $800 for the front end." I held the phone a foot away from my ear, clenched my teeth and squinted.

"Eight hundred dollars!" John yelled. "Eight hundred dollars! Do what you want!" He slammed the phone down. I gently replaced the receiver in its cradle and turned to the expectant-looking man behind the desk.

"He said I could do what I want," I said, "so go ahead with the brakes too." I smiled subtly and fingered the VISA card in my pocket.

I was on my way home when, struck by a sudden urge, I swung past the turn-off and drove to Whippletree Junction, a local shopping destination. I parked in front of a store called The Loom, one of the finest yarn stores in the district. Working brakes give me a lust for sock yarn. I was sure to be demoted from first mate to disgraced crew as soon as I got back to the *Inuksuk* anyway; I might as well be hanged for mutiny as insubordination, and sock yarn would give me something to do while I was in the brig.

Half an hour later I was back in the car clutching a large plastic bag bulging with a brilliant array of sock yarn. Now, what other trouble could I get into on the way home? I stopped at a local gas station, filled up the gas tank and recklessly bought two newspapers and some packaged candy. My VISA card was white-hot with overuse. Flashes of guilt streaked across my psyche, like bird droppings on a newly scrubbed deck. Darling John — so excitable when the VISA bill climbs higher than the mast.

I felt worse when I got back to the *Inuksuk*. John had been worried about me — I'd been gone all day spending money — and he wasn't at all angry. He just turned pale and clutched his chest a little when I told him what I'd spent. Then I did feel terrible. "Would you like to go for a drive, darling?" I asked humbly.

"No, Catherine," John said weakly. "I don't feel up to it."

"Shall I start a pair of socks for you?" I asked. "Pick out any colour you like."

"Whatever colour you like," he said listlessly.

"Would you like to read a newspaper?"

"No."

"Candy?"

"Thanks, but I feel kind of sick. Twelve hundred dollars. I think I'm going to lie down."

I felt low — as low as the barnacles on the hull of the boat. I went over to John and put my arms around him. "I'm sorry, darling," I said. I had danced with the Dark Side of the Force and extinguished the light from my love's bewhiskered face. The Dark Side is the woman's propensity for shopping and the Force is a credit card with money left on it. The Light Side is a man in a marine store. John got up and went into the aft cabin.

"Twelve hundred dollars." His voice floated out to the main saloon. "Do you know what kind of boat parts you could buy with $1,200?" He paused. "A dinghy or a drogue, a second-hand single sideband radio or a tuner ..." His voice trailed off, then reappeared as a ghostly echo with a kind of solemn rhythmic chant. "A solar panel or a watermaker ..." His voice sank into a murmur. "First-aid supplies, emergency provisions for the life raft, a couple of GPSs and a spare radio or two, part of a Sayes rig ..."

"Darling," I called from the main saloon, "are you done?"

"Done? No," John answered mournfully. "A wind generator or a new set of hydraulic controls, one haulout, new plumbing for the water tanks ... There. I'm finished now. Finished," he repeated. "We'll never get offshore at this rate."

I climbed into the aft cabin. "We have the life raft," I ventured. "Life rafts are good. And an EPIRB. EPIRBs are good too. Our wind generator is second-hand, but it seems to work. And the boat floats — it floats like mad. So there," I finished triumphantly. "We're further along than you think."

"Want a radio," he murmured. "Want a single sideband radio." He sighed deeply and lay still. I crept noiselessly out of the cabin, my heart full of pity and guilt. I recalled the story of the poor little girl who, on Christmas Eve, prayed fervently for scarlet ribbons for her ringlets, and unconsciously I drew parallels between the two situations, so similar in their pathos. The parent who overheard the little girl's sobs looked frantically through the village for scarlet ribbons and was unable to find them. In despair, she awaited Christmas morning and the inevitable disappointment of her child. But there was a Christmas miracle. When the little girl awakened, there were scarlet ribbons on her pillow. Angels must have put them there.

I cast my mind back to the many wonderful gifts my husband had given me — gifts that illuminated my life with delight and enchantment like a giant highlighter on the pages of my diary. I remembered fondly the raincoat and the underwater goggles and the electric toothbrush. The book on Vikings chosen thoughtfully and with love, the earrings, the copy of *PCs for Dummies* and the wooden spoon. And over the years, what had I given the man I love in return? A few paltry power tools and some flashlights, socks and underwear and a singing fish.

I took out my VISA card and looked at it. A VISA card, cleverly used, might balance the fear and loathing of debt against the ecstasy of a single sideband radio. If I used the Force to buy boat parts, would I be forgiven?

The next day I paid a surreptitious visit to our neighbour's radio shop. "Fred," I said, "I need your help ..."

Christmas morning I carried the parcel down from storage. John tore the wrappings from the box, then jerked suddenly to a halt. "An Icom radio!" he gasped. "A radio! A radio!" He ripped open the box. The red wrapping ribbons flew to one side and lay curled on the floor like ringlets. Joy radiated from his face, glanced off the shiny black surface of the radio and bounced around the main saloon. The candles flickered, the two-foot-tall tree winked, and I thought I saw the angel in the crèche nod his head a little.

"Darling," I said, "shall I tell you how much it cost?"

"No, my little dumpling," John said. "Don't spoil the moment. Never tell me. I shall imagine it was a gift from the angels."

"*Like scarlet ribbons*," I thought, and I kissed him.

I took my VISA card out of my purse and hid it in my sock drawer with the yarn. Better not to unleash too much Force. A husband is a wonderful and delicate being, and I must use my powers only for good. Then I returned to the main saloon and John, and his radio.

"I used VISA this year too," John said. He handed me a small box. I tore the paper off. "Pearls!" I exclaimed, and I fell into his arms.

We may not have had the wisdom of the Magi, but there is a moral here nonetheless. When spending foolishly — that is, on credit — one is best advised to invest in scarlet ribbons. The great joy is offset by the great debt, it is true, but it is not until the day after Christmas that we will awaken with VISA hangovers. A VISA hangover is mitigated by shiny radios and shiny pearls and the love that we have for each other, even if I do haunt muffler repair shops. Great female philosophers, like Socrates' wife, may disagree with me, but I believe this to be true.

Words of Wisdom

"Granny, how come you have such a little tree on your boat?" asked Alix. "You have little decorations, and little lights too."

"Leaves more room for presents, dear," I said. "Grandpa and I spend all our money on boat parts, so we can't afford a big tree."

"Did you have a tree when you were little?" asked Alix.

"Half a century ago, when Granny was young," I began.

"How old are you, Granny? Eighty?" Alix interrupted.

"No, my darling," I said. "Your granny is a mere child of 48. I know it's hard to believe that someone who looks this good could possibly be 48, but there it is." I sighed. "Great beauty is a terrible responsibility, child. Granny's been cursed with it her entire life. Just ask Grandpa."

"Grandpa," said Alix.

"Hmmmm?" said John.

"Is Granny beautiful?"

"Oh yes," John said hastily. "Beautiful. And she's losing weight, too."

"Thank you, darling," I said. I turned to Alix. "Grandpa is a very wise man. You must always listen to him. Granny always does, except when Grandpa criticizes Granny's cooking."

"I like your cooking," said John, "except perhaps for the onion and apple and prune and bean casserole."

Alix was staying onboard the *Inuksuk* for a day or so while her

162

parents were off gallivanting. We tucked her into the forward cabin every night, and during the day I prepared meals and dispensed grandmotherly wisdom. "Now back to my story, my dear. When Granny was just your age ..."

"I'm eight," Alix said.

"Exactly so, my dear. Just eight. I lived in the Arctic in Churchill, Manitoba, where the polar bears are. We were above the tree line, but there were trees." I laughed. "Oh yes, there were trees. Not an inch taller than five feet, dear, and bent over like old ladies with arthritis. They were all crooked, and there were no branches on the side nearest the water. The Arctic wind blew savagely off Hudson Bay, sweeping south, and my mother told me it blew all the branches off the north side. So you see, my dear, this posed a problem at Christmas, when we had to get a tree."

"Couldn't you buy one at the store?"

"Well, actually, you could. The Hudson's Bay Company used to fly in southern trees, but do you know, they charged six dollars apiece for them. Six dollars was a lot of money in 1963, and Granny's dad said it was highway robbery and he wasn't about to be cheated by the Hudson's Bay Company and at Christmas too, so every year we set out to cut our own tree."

"You did?"

"At a hundred below, if you counted the wind chill factor, with the snow flying sideways into our faces, and the wind slicing through our mittens like needles and our eyelashes frozen together. We didn't dare cry, because the tears would freeze to our faces, and if we stopped to rest our feet would freeze solid. All this was useful training to prepare me for living onboard a boat with Grandpa, dear. Refrigeration, an oven — these things are in my past, and I face food poisoning and my two-burner camp stove without a whimper, just like the Arctic wind and snow up to my armpits. Maybe someday Grandpa will install Granny's oven that we bought cheap at Boater's Exchange. Granny's sister Beth moved up the social ladder to marry a doctor. Granny's sister Gwen moved up the social ladder to practise law. Granny fell in love with Grandpa and learned how to scrape barnacles off a prop while hanging upside down off a ways without getting any seafood caught in her teeth. Granny dodges drips all winter and climbs off a rocking boat onto a swaying dock slick with ice in the winter and bird droppings in the summer. No, Granny hasn't travelled far from her roots.

"In the Arctic, Granny's dad would cut down two Christmas trees and wire them together to make one funny-looking tree in the corner of the living room. Or some years he'd wire the branches of one tree onto the trunk of the other. We had thick coloured lights which worked when the electricity did, and tinsel had just been invented. We'd hang our glass decorations one by one and there it was — a tree to put presents under."

"Do you still have presents?"

"Oh yes, dear, but they've changed. When Granny was a girl I got a Chatty Cathy doll and a Mr. Magoo car that ran on batteries and a book called *Elsie Dinsmore* that had me sobbing for days. You've never met as pathetic a character as Elsie Dinsmore. Her mother was dead, her father ignored her, her governess picked on her, her cousins tormented her and her aunts shunned her. And speaking of tears, when your grandpa gave me that second-hand survival suit, it too brought tears to my eyes. Survival suits are like diamond earrings, dear. You may never encounter the right occasion to wear them, but they're wonderful to have. And just knowing that Grandpa thinks Granny is worth saving if the ship goes down — why, that's as romantic as a whole jewellery case full of sparklers.

"Remember what Granny says, my dear. These words will sustain you in times of travail or distress. Celebrate Christmas even if you have to downsize the tree. Look for a man who gives you meaningful tokens of love, and don't open your lips when you're scraping barnacles off the prop. Merry Christmas, dear."

Not Funny

JOHN AND I were asleep in the aft cabin and our handicapped son Paul was in the forward cabin, when there was a sudden sideways shifting of the boat. The *Inuksuk* slipped silently through the water, then jerked strongly on her mooring lines. I woke up. Groggily I pressed a button on my Mickey Mouse watch. The face lit up with a Kool-Aid blue glow and the hour leaped out at me. Three AM. A buffet of wind struck the rigging and the *Inuksuk* rocked again. I snuggled close to John. "What's up?" I whispered.

"The wind's up," said John. He sounded worried. He struggled out of the bedclothes and put his dressing gown on.

"Where are you going?" I asked.

"I'm going to check the lines," he said. "Stay here." He left the cabin. The boat shifted uneasily, then rolled swiftly toward the dock, rolled back and caught sharply on the lines. John came back to bed and climbed under the covers. "Lines OK," he said. "Go to sleep."

We alternately dozed and lay rigid with our eyes snapped open in the dark. A crunch, as our ferrocement boat smacked sharply into the metal ridges on the dock. The hull shuddered.

I dug my fingers into my husband's shoulder. "I don't like this," I whispered fiercely. John was silent. "What time is it?"

"Five AM." He peered through a porthole into the dark. "Boat's shifted — we've lost one of our lines."

"I'm going to check on Paul," I said. We both scrambled out of the bunk. The boat was rocking from side to side, and hobby-horsing from back to front. There was a shifting in the galley lockers, and the unlit oil lamps swung smoothly. An overhead 110-volt gooseneck lamp on hinges flew at my head out of the dark, then crashed into the wall. I heard the bulb tinkle. Grabbing a bungee cord, I folded the lamp on itself and stumbled over the heaving floor toward the forward cabin. As I reached it the door to the head swung out, then slammed.

"Paul," I whispered, "are you all right?" I reached out my hand and touched his shoulder.

"Mom," he said.

"Go to sleep, baby," I said. "Mommy's here." I staggered to the companionway, climbed the shuddering ladder and stuck my head up through the wildly thrashing hatch. John was standing, legs braced, on the bucking dock.

"Spring line's snapped," he yelled.

"Can you fix it?" I called. The boat lurched toward the floathome directly opposite; the stern line tautened smartly and the dock groaned out loud, heaving against the pylon. I couldn't look.

John fixed the spring and climbed back onboard. Then we both raced around the main saloon, attempting to secure flying missiles. The Christmas tree base had slipped off the top of the TV and hung suspended by a cord around the star. I ripped it free and wedged it, ornaments and all, into a corner of the navigation table. John's old navigation course in its binder shot free of the bookcase and spread itself on the floor. I threw it into a locker and slammed the door shut. I flung myself into the galley and tumbled the drying pots into another locker with a great clatter. The under-table computer counter shot out; John slipped a bungee cord around the table and then caught the electric heater as it shot past on its wheels. He unplugged it and, working quickly so as not to burn his fingers, secured it to the oven handle with another bungee cord. Then, having run flat out of bungee cords, we sat in the main saloon in the dark, our solemn quiet in marked contrast to the colourful riot happening in the cabin.

Gradually the skies lightened, but the seas continued to build. Six-foot waves rolled into the bay with crests on top of them. The *Inuksuk* threw herself in all directions. At eight AM, as the first dawn crept across the bay, our spring line broke again. The boat leaped forward and smashed the cable TV box. John clambered out of the boat to secure the spring and the *Inuksuk* swung over on her side until the edge of the deck touched the dock, and the mast was nearly horizontal. I hustled Paul out of bed, gave him his morning medication, told him to lie down on a settee berth and threw a blanket over top of him.

"Boat!" he crowed, and laughed. Then he grew quiet.

"How are you, Paul?" I asked.

"Sick," he moaned. "Sick," and he burrowed deeper into his blanket. I looked out the porthole. The boat next to us was swinging closer. John climbed back down the companionway.

"John! Look!" I gasped.

"Docks are breaking up," he said grimly. There was a sudden grinding jolt as the boat struck the dock, cement on iron.

At the other end of the dock there was a worried consultation. Ed the Bald eyed the docks, thrashing furiously in a hundred different directions. The dock down at their end was starting to grind apart.

"What about their handicapped boy?" someone said. "Wonder how he's taking it?"

My neighbour was concerned. "I'm going down there to see if Catherine wants to take him off the boat."

"Be careful!" her husband Fred yelled after her. Cautiously she started. The cement groaned and the dock jerked sideways. She fell to her knees, balanced herself, and then began to crawl as the boards bucked under her. She got halfway to the *Inuksuk*, then gave up and crawled back.

"Even if I did make it down there, we'd never get Paul off the boat," she said.

Ed the Bald swayed slightly with the rhythm of the dock, then righted himself. Rain was streaming out of the sky, and even though the wind had died, the seas were working the docks to pieces. "I ain't going down there unless they send up a flare," he said. The ship's bell on Screaming Liver's boat set up a pealing ring as another massive roller pitched his boat sideways. "Brace yourself," Ed said. "Incoming. How in blazes is a guy supposed to take a nap with that bell?"

My neighbour interrupted. "Ed! Fred!" she yelled. "The floathome! It's loose again!" The two men shot across the dock to grab lines. "Watch my dog," Ed said, as he disappeared with the other men to wrestle with the floathome.

Onboard the *Inuksuk*, incongruously, the cell phone rang. Lurching from side to side, I made my way to the companionway entrance and braced myself on the ladder to clutch the phone. We were about to die, but reception is better under the hatch.

Paul moaned slightly and turned under his blanket. "Sick," he said again, then fell silent.

"Hello?" I said, and grabbed the ladder as the boat threw herself sideways.

"Call-out," said a cheerful voice. "How are you this morning?"

"Not very good," I said.

As I hung up, I could see part of Pier 66 floating past. John jumped from the dock to the boat and hurriedly began to dig through the deck box. "Looking for a shackle," he said. "Our finger's apart at the dock end."

"Murray's boat is too close," I yelled.

"His finger is broken too," he said. "Need shackles to fix them."

German Bob, dressed in boots and cords and a sweater, stood on the deck of his thrashing cutter looking almost nonchalant, then lowered himself gracefully onto the dock to join the group of men there fighting to do repairs. I returned to the main saloon and sat across from my son, both of us queasy and solemn. It was dark in the cabin, and cold. The lamps creaked as they swung back and forth. I gritted my teeth and set about waiting out the storm.

By noon the water was flat as glass. We were pale and shaken, but the boat had suffered nothing worse than a few gouges in the hull and a twisted cleat. The men finished repairs to the docks, and we started to feel more optimistic. Paul and I sat up, and all three of us ate a little.

Our neighbour came to visit. "How did Paul make out?" she asked. "We were worried about him — your boat was really moving."

"Not funny," Paul said mournfully. "Not funny."

"Honey," I said, "that about sums it up."

Bed and a Bath

It all began when the Australian Dooks came to Canada. We met Rob and Norma in the lobby of their upscale hotel in Vancouver, nearly giving them heart failure as they walked into the lobby and were greeted by a large and motley group of Dooks. There was Lisa and Mikey and Lito and John and me, all of us waving and shouting. In the name of hospitality we whisked them into our beat-up Oldsmobile and insisted they come to Cowichan Bay to stay with us.

Rob cast a longing eye back at the hotel as we left. "Do you have a bathtub?" he asked wistfully.

"Heavens, no," I laughed lightly. "But our shower is clean — last week, wasn't it, darling? And we have lots of hot water. Unless we run out." Rob was very quiet on the trip over. Probably jet lag.

When we got to the boat, Rob, tall as a tree, had to fold himself a little to fit into the main saloon. I waved my hand grandly toward the V-berth in the forward cabin. "One and a half berths," I said. "We can fit both of you in there."

Norma smiled uncertainly. "My — it's a snug little cabin, isn't it?" she said weakly.

Rob ducked his head into the cabin. "I won't fit," he said flatly. "Is there a hotel nearby?"

"Well, yes," said John. "The Wessex."

"Do they have bathtubs?" asked Rob.

We had a marvellous visit, and Rob said the Wessex was worth every penny.

The following summer my parents drove down from the Northwest Territories. "You can stay with us," I said happily over cups of coffee in the main saloon. My mother braced herself as a passing powerboat rocked us sideways.

Dad cleared his throat. "It's a kind offer," he began.

"But we're too old to stay on a boat, dear," Mom said. "We've checked into the Wessex."

"Nice rooms," said Dad.

"And they don't move," said Mom firmly. She smiled. "Besides, I like a nice bath."

In the fall, my friend Wilma and her husband Tim came to the boat. "The forward cabin is yours anytime you want it," I said. "Just move right in."

"Now, Catherine," said Wilma, "I'm not saying I'm claustrophobic, but do you remember the time in Chief's sweatlodge when I fainted and had to be dragged out by the armpits? Your forward cabin is too small. But I would like to take a bath." She looked around expectantly.

"Well, we've got a great shower," I said. "Just duck into the head and wedge yourself into this corner here, reach behind you and hold this wand over your head and voila!" Wilma smiled politely.

"I think we'll check into the Wessex," she said, "if it's all the same to you."

My Aunt Cecily drove up from Victoria. "I'd love to stay onboard," she said, "but I'm waiting for hip-replacement surgery."

"We know a great hotel," I said. "Just down the street."

Everyone had left. It was a rotten day. The head impeller had broken and John had fought valiantly to fix it. The pipes were starting to smell funny — probably they'd need to be changed soon, but that was a major operation and would involve taking the cabin wall apart. The valves to the steel water tanks were leaking, or perhaps the overflow hoses were siphoning, and the bilge pump had been steadily dumping fresh water into the ocean for a week. We'd run out of water halfway through the dishes again that morning. The forward cabin was filled with debris left over from Christmas and it was starting to filter its way back to the aft cabin.

John and I went for a walk. We felt the need of fresh air and wide open spaces. As we walked arm in arm down the road, I noticed that our neighbours looked like us — or perhaps we looked like our neighbours. Cowichan Bay residents look and smell a particular way — rumpled, with an aroma of paint and thinner and mould and diesel. The grottiness of Cowichan Bay felt settled into our bones. We strolled past the Wessex, then stopped and looked back.

"John," I said, "everyone says it's a nice place to stay." John didn't say anything.

"They have clean bathtubs," I said. "Let's check into the Wessex."

"What for?" said John.

"Darling," I said, "our entire extended family has checked into the Wessex. I think we should investigate it further. I have a dream — that someday I can stretch out in all directions on a bed, and that someday I will sit in a bathtub until I am wrinkly all over." I sighed.

"Perhaps one day you will," said John. "Perhaps one day all your visions of happiness will come true at the Wessex."

"Both of us are dreamers, my darling," I said. "You want to go offshore, and I want to check into the local hotel. Who knows what the future holds? Who knows what happiness awaits us? Next payday. They have cable."

"Done," said John.

Mooring Buoy Drama

"I<small>T WASN'T SO</small> bad," I told my neighbour one spring morning at the Starfish Studio. I ran my yarn delicately around my needles and began the first round of another sock — blue with a pattern this time.

"What was it like?" she asked.

"We circled it just like a wild dog after rotting meat, desperation and cunning stamped all over our faces."

"Good heavens!" she gasped.

"I speak, of course, of a mooring buoy," I said placidly. "Now where was I? Knit one, purl one." I shifted slightly in my chair and took a sip of tea from a paper cup. "We were at the Three Sisters Islands in Ganges Harbour visiting Clive and his wife. We knew they'd be glad to see us, especially if we didn't rip their mooring buoy out by the roots and drag it away with us."

"How much does the *Inuksuk* weigh?" asked my neighbour.

"Sixty thousand pounds," I said brightly. "Darn it all, I dropped a stitch. Now where was I? The *Inuksuk* doesn't stop on a dime, you know. In fact, you wouldn't get change from a $100 bill. We prowled heavily through the water, frightening seals and seabirds, the crew, and Clive and his good wife. John stood bravely at the helm, and I stood courageously at the bow with a pike pole in my whitened fist. Jean-Paul spent eight years in the South Pacific and he knows everything. He lounged in the cockpit and waited for us to give up and ask his advice. First pass, we shot past the mooring buoy at three knots. Second pass, John threw the engine slap into neutral 100 feet from the mark."

"And how fast did you shoot past it the second time?" asked my neighbour.

"About two and a half knots," I said calmly. "We nearly beached ourselves on their island. Pass me that cream?"

"Goodness," said my neighbour. "Have you and John ever used a mooring buoy before?"

"Oh no," I said. "Every voyage with John is an adventure. Ed the Bald told me that years ago the first time I went out sailing with John, and now I know it's true."

"What happened then?" asked my neighbour.

"Ferociously we bore down on the mooring buoy for the third time. The current caught us, and the bow of the *Inuksuk* stopped smack on the buoy. Confidently I snaked the pike pole down — down I knelt — down farther — I flattened myself on the deck, caught the ring with the pike pole and pulled. Nothing happened. I pulled again. The ring did not ascend magically into my hand. Instead, it sulked in the water and sneered at me. I made helpless noises and flapped frantically to John — semaphore, I think — 'Abort mission ... return to Cowichan Bay ... Reverse ... Advise immediately ... Forward.'

"Jean-Paul advanced to the bow, quietly as a shadow, and silently straightened the bow line down the length of the deck. 'Pull the buoy down the port side with the pole,' he said softly. Lying flat on his belly amidships, he threaded the line neatly through the ring with his one good hand, then leaped to his feet, pulled stoutly and deftly tied off the end of the line. The *Inuksuk* shuddered to a halt, the mooring buoy held, and Clive and his wife came roaring out in their little runabout to pick us up.

"Clive apologized later for his unseamanlike docking on the island, because he came in bow first and fended the dock off with his feet, but we didn't feel we were in a position to be scornful. Do you like this pattern?" I held up my knitting.

"Lovely," said my neighbour. "I really should do the second sock to that pair I started three years ago, but I think instead I'll trade Fred in for a man with one leg."

"Did you ever have trouble using mooring buoys?" I asked.

"Oh no," she said. "Of course the rings never came up, and we never got them on the first try — especially with people watching — but they're really not bad once you get used to them. Mooring buoys are like men," she said.

"You mean they look nice at a distance but when you get up close you realize they never ask for directions and they scorn any food with sauce on it except beans?" I asked. We both laughed. "They like to do their own repairs, and there's a three-year gap between when you say, 'Honey, we don't have an oven,' and they install one? They're funny and adorable and they dream about impossible adventures and they never get mad when you buy them boat parts, even if they're the wrong size? They think you're beautiful even when there is evidence to the contrary? They buy you a coast guard auxiliary uniform for your birthday?"

"Well, no, but there are similarities. Mooring buoys aren't as clever as my Fred, or as romantic, or as impractical, but they really aren't so bad. They take some getting used to, but you just have to know how to handle them, after all," she said. "Mooring buoys and men both."

One More Journey

W E ARE ABOUT to depart for Ganges Harbour again, Jean-Paul and Angéique and John and I. Ed the Bald says Jean-Paul is the only resident of Cowichan Bay crazy enough to go out with us. True, he is a little eccentric. He holds up his artificial hand and hisses, "I use' to be right handed, but I switch," then laughs with terrifying wildness. This frightens everyone but his young daughter, who has her father well under control.

The engine starts with a roar. John and I make our way to the stern of the boat to admire the saucy jets of water that spurt out of the exhaust.

The neighbours gather to see us off. "Heading out?" yells German Bob from the deck of his boat. "I'll stand by my radio, John." He cups his hands to his mouth and bellows, "The Dooks are going out. Call the coast guard now and save trouble later." He chuckles and goes below.

Geoff leans down from the deck of the *Shogun*. "Don't hit my boat," he jokes. When John tells him I'll have the wheel this time, he ceases smiling. "Marilyn, get me a pike pole," he says over his shoulder.

Screaming Liver, sailing past toward the bay, waves a beer can in greeting. On the dock my neighbour hugs me. "Are you sure you have my cell phone number?" she asks. "Al's cell phone number too? Fred's at work. You can get him there until 4:30."

Ed the Bald grins wickedly. "If John sinks the boat, think of the material you'll have for your next book, Catherine," he says. "Those adventure stories about near-death are best-sellers."

"Thanks a lot, Ed," says John.

Stafford the Respectable claps Ed the Bald on the shoulder. "They'll be all right," he says. "Angelique's onboard this trip."

I jump into the cockpit. Jean-Paul unties the thick mooring lines. He climbs aboard. The *Inuksuk* hangs heavily in the water, as if currents and tides and motors mean nothing.

John gives me the wheel. The diesel engine blasts into forward and our great boat noses slowly around the corner of the dock. I miss that edge, there, and the half-floating, half-sunken tugboat to starboard, and as I turn slowly to port I miss the old fuel barge and the sullen log breakwater. I miss the *Shogun* by yards. I am filled with elation. Jean-Paul snorts — a sound halfway between "About time she's taken us away from the dock," and "Angelique could have done it without the coaching," but I ignore him. How can my skills be compared with those of Angelique? She's been onboard a boat a hundred percent of her life and I've mastered a few nautical skills in the last ten percent of mine.

Sunshine bleaches the cockpit and floods over the deck. The air is without movement. A few clouds dust the sky. Jean-Paul sits in the cockpit with his arms around his little daughter. John steers a straight course toward Ganges Harbour.

I stand firmly in the cockpit with our big stone boat under my feet. The *Inuksuk* is ready for anything the ocean has to offer, and the day is full of possibilities. Around the next point might lie adventure, but I am ready. You see, my grandma once told me that if you love somebody and they love you, you can face anything. Our neighbours like us, I know. We're not that sure about German Bob, but he seems to tolerate us. And we like our neighbours, or most of them; with the kind of unstinting, unmeasured affection we've experienced, how could we not launch into the unknown with courage? And on this trip, I'm taking with me two friends and my own true love.

A new page has turned over in our logbook. I am enjoying myself.

Afterword: Looking Forward, Looking Back

There have been many changes in the past year, but some things remain the same. Screaming Liver still has half a paint job on his cutter. He blew out a sail last week, but he's the happiest man on the dock. It must be all that beer. Ed the Bald is a pack rat yet. He had just fixed the soft spots in his hull when his head broke down, so he's saving up money to fix it. Stafford the Respectable, now that it's spring, has taken to washing the walls of his floathome, to the incredulous amusement of his neighbours. Iron Mike is growing chives and petunias as well as tomatoes this year.

Older-Than-Dirt Don has moved into a trailer in Duncan, still not admitting that his tiny trimaran was not fit to go offshore. He had planned to sail it to Australia, then was diagnosed with cancer and had to put off his trip. He triumphantly survived the cancer and gave up on the notion of travel. This is the only documented case anywhere of cancer saving someone's life.

German Bob is predicting the end of the world. Other John moved off his boat into a house nearby. Fred still doesn't have an engine, but he lives in hope; my neighbour grows geraniums and goes for walks and is cheerful despite Fred, she says, but we all know they are devoted to each other. She has a gift for happiness. Buddy the cat developed diabetes and had to be put down. Nika the pit bull doesn't bark as much now that Buddy's gone.

William of the Cowichan Bay Coast Guard Auxiliary was team leader last time we went out and, even though we nearly collided with some rocks, his efficient leadership left our jaws dropped in spontaneous shock. Not once did he call for a beverage. Not once did he crack a joke or wave a spotlight frivolously. He is a man who lives up to the role allotted him; given lesser responsibilities he is a master of hilarious sabotage. We are considering rallying behind him for district manager. William for King! The possibilities are boggling.

I found a job. John is rubbing his hands and looking up boat parts in catalogues.

Jean-Paul is more silent than ever and devotes himself to his daughter and his boat. Endis died at 26. She was not as lucky as Older-Than-Dirt Don. She died in the spring, after a courageous struggle with a vicious cancer. She did not die alone. The congregation of an Anglican church and members of the Canadian Cancer Society stood quietly alongside the family, while her doctors and nurses fought hard for her life. We all visited and brought papaya juice to remind her of her island so far away and we collected money to pay for her morphine. And we cried. Once, after we'd wept together, she said, "I am very lucky. God has given me a husband, a daughter, a family, good friends and a boat." She died on a borrowed bed, and we cremated her in a second-hand dress. She had nothing but love. And that is everything.

Someday John and I will sail to Vanuatu. There we will visit with Jean-Paul and Angelique, and we will think of Endis. She is not gone. She is where the winds are.

Catherine Dook was born in Yellowknife, Northwest Territories, and raised in Churchill, Manitoba. She has taught school across the north and met her husband, John, while she was teaching in Nunavut. Until she met John, the only boat she'd been on was a ferry across the Mackenzie River. John loved boats and the sea, and when he and Catherine married in 1996, she agreed to embark upon a new life: living aboard their 44-foot sailboat *Inuksuk*.

Catherine's stories have appeared in *Boat Journal* and *Nor'westing* magazines. Her first book of tales about liveaboard life, published in 2001, is called *"Darling, Call the Coast Guard, We're on Fire Again!"*